"A timely and compelling book with essential guidance on racism and equity. This book contains today's must-have insight on two vital, yet often misunderstood, roles on the road to racial equity: *allies and advocates*. Highlighting how the unprecedented events of 2020 have further underscored the urgency for equity, Allies and Advocates serves as a roadmap to guide the steps and responsibilities each of us hold toward making racial equity a reality. It is a crucial read for all who seek to embrace anti-racism."

—Dr. Lauren R. Powell, National Health Equity Leader, President & CEO, The Equitist

"It has been my privilege to have known and worked with Ms. Cabral for several years. The work that it takes to drive inclusion and belonging is not only a mission to change minds but also to change hearts and behaviors. This book is essential not only for those who would like to become more inclusive leaders but also for those who have been enlightened by the events of these turbulent times. There are few people that I have seen as good as Ms. Cabral at understanding what it takes to drive leaders to action on topics that many would find uncomfortable. As leaders, it is our responsibility to do what's best for our organizations but also its employees and their communities. This book provides a step-by-step guide for those who want to take action around D&I but do not know what to do next. That kind of clarity is beneficial regardless of where you are on your D&I journey."

—Reginald J. Miller, VP, Global Chief Diversity, Equity, & Inclusion Officer, McDonalds

Allies

and

Advocates

Allies
and
Advocates

CREATING AN **INCLUSIVE**
AND **EQUITABLE CULTURE**

AMBER CABRAL

WILEY

For general information on our other products and services or for technical support, please contact our Customer Care Department within the United States at (800) 762-2974, outside the United States at (317) 572-3993 or fax (317) 572-4002.

Wiley publishes in a variety of print and electronic formats and by print-on-demand. Some material included with standard print versions of this book may not be included in e-books or in print-on-demand. If this book refers to media such as a CD or DVD that is not included in the version you purchased, you may download this material at http://booksupport.wiley.com. For more information about Wiley products, visit www.wiley.com.

Library of Congress Cataloging-in-Publication Data is Available:

ISBN 9781119772934 (Hardcover)
ISBN 9781119772958 (ePDF)
ISBN 9781119772941 (ePub)

Cover Design: Paul Mccarthy
Cover Photograph: Danielle Finney
Graphic art design: Malgosia Kostecka of www.illumistories.com

Printed in the United States of America

SKY10024900_021121

To Rin—the most magical person I know.

You can have whatever you want.

Contents

Acknowledgments

Amanda Miller Littlejohn for far too many things, but mostly for helping me redefine normal

Christopher Parker Djordje for your friendship, trust, and patience with my moods

Aimee L. Strang for leaning in and always feeding the writer

Dr. Kamasi Hill for checking my knowledge

Malgosia Kostecka for your incredible illustrations to help bring this content to life

Jonathan M. Kester, Esq., for your legal mind and forever friendship

Everyone in the MBK group chat + Theo and Cher Nicholson— thank you for always giving me shelter (both literally and figuratively), cheering me on, and giving me space to celebrate the wins

Kirstie Perry, RaSheem Barnett, Carey T. Jones, Joshua Spivey, Conrad Woody, and Keila Hill-Trawick for believing in me even when I had doubt

Pamela and James Estes

Michelle Baker

Antonio Cabral

Introduction

First things first, relax. Put your shoulders down, quiet the anxiety in the pit of your stomach, and take a deep breath. This book is a learning tool. You will meet a lot of challenging and complex information, ideas, and perspectives aimed at helping you figure out how you can move justice and equity forward. The best way to position yourself in context to this material is as a learner in a virtual classroom where you can feel safe bringing your curiosity, showcase your eagerness to learn, and bravely reconsider your existing ideas. This is a "safe space," as folks say. This book isn't about shaming or lecturing you to do or be better. Likely if you picked up this book, you already have had some bout with these feelings. These feelings are normal, especially if you are new to this work.

This book is about presenting information to help you figure out your place in what is a very long movement toward equity for oppressed people. Throughout these pages I invite you to do the work to move justice and equity forward. We explore some history for context on why oppression is so deeply entrenched in our identities. We cover language because, as my best friend always likes say, "Words mean things." You will understand why some words are triggering for you and put you on the defensive. You will discover that a lot of the behaviors you are doing are flat-out wrong and be armed with the right behaviors to move forward.

For those of you who think you've got it but are looking for ways to check your friends and family, I have a bit of mixed news. You don't have it. No one does. This book will teach you how to get comfortable with that fact and still learn how to maneuver and push allyship and equity forward. So, if you think you've got it and know, settle in; there will be a lot of nods of agreement but likely still many eye-opening perspectives to lean on as you continue on your allyship journey.

In some ways I consider this book foundational; it gives the basic things you need to understand to communicate with others about allyship and advocacy responsibly. In many ways this book only scratches the surface because inclusion work is ever evolving and has such a rich history that capturing its many facets is virtually impossible. If you are new to this work, consider this a starting place; if you are farther along in allyship and advocacy, consider this a rich refresher.

Thinking of this as a refresher reminds me of the instructions for proper handwashing that flooded the internet when the United States began shutting down due to the coronavirus in March 2020. Likely you knew how to wash your hands, and likely you already washed your hands several times a day. Then the incessant reminders to wash and the "proper handwashing" signs took over, and you had to remind yourself of the bits you had gotten lazy about in your routine. Always, every time, rub the back of one hand with the palm of the other. Always get under the nails. Always use the whole 20 seconds. Don't let routine lull you into lax habits. This work is the same. It can feel like a lot of routine, but relaxing into that routine makes room for the status quo, and that just ain't enough. When leaning into this work, we need to apply the same diligence that we apply to handwashing during a pandemic.

In this book you will learn what to do and how to be, but you will be compelled to action by your own sense of self rather than being convinced or directed by the text. I am not here to convince you. My expectation is that if you are at the point of wanting to call yourself an ally and wanting to know how to be an advocate for others, you are convinced that there need to be changes. I give you the information you need to find your own reasons to act. I want you to discover in these pages the reasons why you cannot sideline this work and why you absolutely have to show up. I want you to discover why you are called to be an ally for others in your own words. That way when someone asks you why it matters, you can speak from a place of candor and vulnerability that gives depth and life to why this work is important. Certainly, you can memorize stats and know the data—I consume copious amounts of data and statistics so I can do my job well. It is for that reason that I can tell you that data doesn't move things forward. Stories do. People who are motivated to action by cause, by purpose, by excitement, by infection—that is what makes change. When people feel it. This book is going to lean into the parts of this work that gets into your bones. There will be emotion. This work is, after all, about our humanity, our lives, and how to make room for the survival of us all.

That said, there is a lot of emotional and difficult history and background in this book. I want to establish some ground rules to help you move through it and get the most out of the material presented.

First, do not take anything in this book personally. Everything in this book is useful, but you have to put yourself in the state of mind where you are able to receive it and be present to the message without being consumed by your personal response. This is not to say that I want you to be numb; rather, feel your feelings and take a break if you need to—but do not stop. Almost everything in this book is about identity, so at times it will be easy to see yourself in the material and get offended. Push those feelings aside. Take a walk if it helps. Keep in mind that these topics are things we typically dance around. It makes sense to feel some discomfort when exploring the racism, police brutality, and social injustices that are being covered openly in the news right now. Even though discussing these things may feel strange and awkward, we all know times are changing. Let's meet the moment with bravery.

Second, on bravery: It is essential for inclusion and antiracism work. Usually for us to be brave in a space, we need a sense of confidence about our identity and a sense of purpose. Right now, you might feel very brave in a number of ways but not necessarily as it relates to being an ally and an advocate for others. That's okay. Bravery is a muscle that can be built, and this book will help you to build it. By learning what being an ally means and how to identify behaviors and habits for yourself that communicate your bravery and confidence to others, you will develop the confidence you need to be brave. As you move through the chapters of this book and identify your own sense of purpose for leaning into this work, your bravery will strengthen.

Third, we are all on the same team. Racial equity, dismantling systemic oppression, physical and psychological safety, and creating an inclusive world require teamwork. If you want any of those things, then we are in this together. Right now you might not be sure you understand the obstacles that keep people from having racial equity, feeling safe or included or why people face systemic oppression, that's okay. We will cover those topics. If you want those things for yourself and everyone else, consider us teammates—even when I share something that doesn't feel so good to read.

Fourth, inclusion and diversity work (which includes antiracism work) consumes energy and makes you think. Throughout this book there are places for you to reflect on your own thoughts and ideas about the content. I ask questions for you to consider and ask that you think about how the information connects to your own experience. Remember, inclusion and diversity work is people work, so I want you, my fellow person, to take time to be thoughtful about how the work shows up in your own life. Additionally, I share tips and tactics to help you navigate certain common encounters and even manage your emotions and energy.

Last, this work requires vulnerability and candor. Inclusion touches everything so we are going to cover: real-life circumstances, actual missteps, relevant examples, and tactics. We are keeping it real here. We won't need to make up scenarios or encounters because when it comes to inclusion work, there is plenty in the real world to draw from. I am going to be candid and cover some topics that may feel awkward. I use and define words we usually are nervous about, such as racism and white supremacy. There is no way to discuss the ways you can show up and do the work of allyship and advocacy without explicitly talking about the things our comfort zones sometimes ask us to avoid. I am going to share with vulnerability so you are able to understand how the work comes to life outside of these pages. In the spirit of keeping it real, as we work through these pages, I am going to challenge you to answer the questions posed to you with the level of vulnerability and candor necessary to help you move the work forward.

This book is a safe space and a learning space, but it also is a challenging one. We cover a lot of material in very simple ways. My goal is to give you a rich starting point from which to begin or accelerate your steps toward allyship. From new concepts and terms to bravely learning to lean into the bold behaviors necessary for being an ally and an advocate, you are in for an informative and emotional ride. I am so excited that you are joining me on this journey.

This book is divided into three parts. Part I focuses on allyship and advocacy and explains the behaviors necessary to being an ally and an advocate. Part II is about the language of inclusion. A lot of terms and topics fall under the umbrella of inclusion and equity, so this part provides a basic understanding of terms and topics you may encounter on your journey to allyship and advocacy. Part III is about the importance of starting with yourself when looking for ways to be an ally or an advocate. Allyship and advocacy require not only awareness but also a willingness to work on your own perspectives.

Let's get started.

Allies
and
Advocates

1 The Current Landscape

The two most common questions I encounter while teaching since the Black Lives Matter protests began in May after the killing of George Floyd in Minneapolis on May 25, 2020, are: "How did racial inequity become such a big problem?" and "Why are these protests happening now?" They are both such important questions that, despite their simplicity, quite a bit of background and context is required to fully understand the answers. As you are likely wondering these things yourself in your work to be an ally and an advocate for others, I'm going to paint a full picture of "how we got here" and "why these protests are happening right now."

I want to start by discussing the current global landscape and its impact. There are a lot of global shifts happening in the world at the same time—a global pandemic, protests against racial justice, climate change, changes in the political landscape, and much, much more. I think everyone around the globe would agree that 2020 has been a hell of a year. The first two months of the year were probably the closest to what many of us would call "normal," and they were still pretty eventful. Just to recap, here are a few things that happened in the first 60 days of 2020 around the globe:

- Wild bush fires destroyed millions of acres, homes, and wildlife in Australia.
- Prince Harry and Meghan Markle announced they were stepping down from their royal duties.
- A Ukrainian flight crashed in Tehran, Iran, killing all 176 passengers on board.
- Kobe Bryant and his daughter Gigi Bryant, along with seven others, died in a helicopter crash in California.

- The United Kingdom exited the European Union, making Brexit a reality.
- Donald J. Trump, president of the United States, impeached by the House of Representatives, was acquitted on impeachment charges by the Senate.
- Disgraced Hollywood producer Harvey Weinstein, known for *Pulp Fiction* and *Shakespeare in Love,* was convicted of third-degree rape and first-degree criminal sexual acts.

Wild, right? Some of those things feel like they happened years ago, and that's not including all the coronavirus news that happened in that same window of time. In January 2020, the World Health Organization (WHO) was notified about 2019-nCoV virus in China. A couple of weeks later, China reported its first coronavirus death, and by the end of January, the city of Wuhan in Hubei Province in China was on a complete lockdown. By mid-February, WHO officially named the 2019-nCoV disease the name we all know now, COVID-19, and nations around the world began to take notice as concerns about the virus's reach and its severity dominated news cycles. In March, we saw European nations entering varying phases of lockdown to control the virus, and on March 11, 2020, WHO declared COVID-19 a global pandemic.

I remember the moment when the virus got real for me. I was in London in mid-February on what would turn out to be my last business trip of the year. The day of my departure, my client let me know fears of the coronavirus global pandemic had led to the postponement of our March engagement in Lisbon. By February 20, all work my business had booked for 2020 was either postponed or canceled altogether. In a week, my business went from being on track to have the most successful year ever to zero dollars and a commitment to my staff that I would figure it out and not let them go. Suddenly I was trying to figure out rent and health insurance and keeping the business running on the few invoices we had still waiting on payment. It was terrifying.

Everyone has a story, though, as the global pandemic is affecting everyone at the same time and in different ways.

Take a few moments and consider how your life has changed since the global pandemic. Answer the following questions:

- How has coronavirus changed the way you live?
- What are some concerns you have as a result of the global pandemic?

- How has coronavirus changed how you see the world?
- What are some new things you have learned, big or small, as a result of coronavirus?
- How has the global pandemic affected your loved ones?

Since the onset of the pandemic, some things are uncomfortable, like not being able to get a haircut or go to the gym, and even having air travel restricted. I'm a woman with short hair who traveled a lot for business. I am currently living in DC with a hairstylist in Detroit. This was no problem when I was on the road 85% of the time. I'd plan for a weekend layover in Detroit, get my hair done, and continue on with my life. Having a hairstylist in Detroit, a doctor in Dallas, and a dentist in Atlanta seems silly and irresponsible now that air travel isn't exactly safe. In reality, though, these are just inconveniences. I will survive with a bit of new growth and skipping my annual checkup.

The coronavirus has changed the world in other very remarkable and life-altering ways. The whole world is feeling it, and when you consider that there are over 7 billion people on the planet, it's mind blowing that something we can't see with our naked eyes can have such a massive impact. Some of the major changes include these:

- Had you ever heard of "social distancing" or "physical distancing" before the coronavirus? I certainly hadn't. As a result of the coronavirus, we now have an entirely new language around how we should behave. Social distancing, wearing your mask, and washing your hands constantly are a part of everyday life.
- What about "essential workers"? Prior to coronavirus, I would have described an essential worker as someone who worked in a hospital or someone that works in a power plant. Today we also think of essential workers as people who help grocery stores run, people who keep transportation moving, both in and out of the country, and even people who work in food plants.
- There have been major economic impacts as a result of the coronavirus, including sweeping layoffs and furloughs resulting in millions of people in the United States needing unemployment assistance. The stock market has been volatile, and the government has been a part of a constant conversation about what needs to happen to stimulate the economy and support people and business owners who are unable to work.

- Alarming rates of unexpected illness and death have come with the coronavirus. At the time of this writing, over half a million people had died from the virus and there were over 14 million confirmed cases globally. People are losing friends and family and not even having the chance to say good-bye. I have personally lost a number of close friends and some distant family members due to coronavirus.

- That leads me to health system strain. We have heard a lot about how we need to be at home, "sheltering in place" so we can reduce the spread of the virus and slow the burden on our health system. Almost nightly there are reports of hospital units in areas hit by a surge in cases being at capacity for patients. When a facility is at capacity, that means it cannot take on more patients, even those with other illnesses, and there is additional pressure put on the hospital staff.

- Had you ever heard of PPE before this pandemic? PPE stands for personal protective equipment. It includes the gear that medical staff need to wear to ensure they do not catch the coronavirus when they come in contact with someone with the virus who needs treatment. PPE includes masks, gloves, and face shields. When the coronavirus first hit the United States and everyone was afraid to catch it, it was virtually impossible to find PPE as well as other things that help people stay safe and keep things clean, like hand sanitizer and disinfectant wipes.

- On the mental health front, there have been reports of increased levels of stress-induced anxiety, depression, and even domestic abuse since the onset of the pandemic. People are less able to get the help they need with cities shutting down and people sheltering in place to reduce the spread of the virus.

- Children are at home with parents full-time; in some cases, parents have had to figure out how to balance doing their jobs while making sure their children are participating in virtual learning. As much as we may love our families, everyone needs a little time apart or with their friends. People are feeling the emotional strain of not being able to manage their relationships as they could pre-pandemic.

- Conversely, some people are sheltering in place alone. Instead of feeling the psychological strain of being around a lot of people, they have strong feelings of loneliness and isolation. I am a single woman, living in a new city, with no children. The isolation and loneliness for me during the pandemic has been palpable.

No matter your circumstances, you are feeling something as a result of the many changes to everyday life that have come with COVID-19, and one thing is for sure—everyone is trying to make the best of the new environment.

Let's examine for a moment what pandemic life might be like if you are a member of an underrepresented group. An underrepresented racial and ethnic group is a group of people who make up a smaller percentage of a specific population. In this case, let's zoom in on the American population. Underrepresented racial and ethnic groups in the United States include Black or African Americans, Asian Americans, Hispanic or Latinx people, Native Americans, and Native Hawaiians. Underrepresented racial groups in the United States have an even greater set of impacts due to the onset of the global pandemic.

NOTE "Latinx" refers to both Latinos and Latinas. Since "Latino" and "Latina" connote male and female respectively, the "x" in Latinx includes all genders of the Latin community. We discuss this more in Part II of the book.

- Asian Americans are experiencing xenophobia. Xenophobia is dislike or prejudice toward people from another country—or people who appear to be from another country. Since the coronavirus is thought to have begun in China, Asian Americans have reported mistreatment from other Americans, including being told they are nasty, must have the virus, or to "go back where they came from." Some of our Asian American friends and colleagues have had encounters that have escalated into violence because some feel that an Asian appearance is enough to assume that a person is a carrier of COVID-19. (It is important to note that xenophobia is not unique to the United States; it is a global phenomenon. In fact, in China, there have been reports that anyone who is not Chinese has been met with prejudice because in China people believe the virus was brought in by someone who is not Chinese.)
- Another term that is being used in regard to COVID-19 is "community spread." "Community spread" refers to people being infected with the virus in a particular area, often not knowing how they contracted it. Members of underrepresented racial groups have been seeing higher rates of community spread than members of White communities.

- Marginalized people also tend to work many of the jobs we now call "essential," like meat plant workers and bus drivers, which puts them in contact with more people and increases their opportunity for exposure to the virus. The essential jobs are ones that cannot be done remotely, so such workers have to put themselves at risk by being in contact with other people. Only 16.2% of Hispanic workers and 19.7% of Black workers can telework, according to the Economy Policy Institute.[1]

- Unemployment has spiked during the pandemic. We know that the novel coronavirus has impacted many jobs, but many of the entry-level and blue-collar jobs that have been impacted are largely worked by people in marginalized groups. As a result, people who are in marginalized groups are more likely to be unemployed during the pandemic.

- With job loss on the rise, so is the loss of health coverage. Thus, many in underrepresented racial groups who lost their jobs also lost their health coverage. Underrepresented racial groups tend to be underinsured when compared to White people in general, so the pandemic-driven layoffs have only made the health coverage situation worse. A lack of health insurance often results in individuals choosing to delay care until their health situation is critical. In the case of COVID-19, the decision to delay care can be a fatal one.

- In the first few months of the pandemic, some obstacles to testing hit underrepresented groups in particular: First, testing required a doctor's order—which, for many people, means they need to have health insurance, a problem we covered in the previous bullet point. Second, testing sites did not ensure equitable access. Test sites were drive-up, with long lines that were obstacles for those without vehicles or who still had jobs to report to. Early on, test sites were also not placed in the communities where marginalized people live, so they had to travel to get to testing.

- Underrepresented racial minorities are more likely to live in multigenerational households, meaning there might be children,

---

[1] Elise Gould and Heidi Shierholz, "Not Everybody Can Work from Home: Black and Hispanic Workers Are Much Less Likely to Be Able to Telework," *Working Economics Blog*, Economic Policy Institute, March 19, 2020, https://www.epi.org/blog/black-and-hispanic-workers-are-much-less-likely-to-be-able-to-work-from-home/

parents, and grandparents all living in the same home. When a number of people live in a home, the ability for those in the home to adhere to social or physical distancing, should someone get sick, is reduced. As a result, early reporting showed that entire families were getting ill after one person brought the virus into the home.

NOTE I use the term "underrepresented" or "marginalized" instead of "minority." Why? Because the root word of minority is "minor," which suggests that the people who are part of that group do not have major impact. We discuss this more in Part II of the book.

Without a doubt, pandemic life is likely to be tougher for underrepresented racial groups in the United States. This is still only part of the picture though. To get to the answers to the questions I hear most often—"How did we get here?" and "Why are these protests happening now?"—we need to zoom in a bit more and focus on the Black or African American population. How different might surviving a pandemic be for members of this group? In addition to facing all of the experiences described in the earlier bullet points,

- Black or African American people are estimated to have the highest rate of coronavirus infections. Their likelihood of being infected is three to six times that of White Americans.
- The death rate for Black or African American people who contract the novel coronavirus is the highest of all racial groups.
- The unemployment rate for Black or African American people during the pandemic is higher than for all other racial groups.
- African Americans start out with health outcomes that are disproportionately poor when compared to White Americans. The Black and African American population is inherently sicker. These health inequities are the result of reduced access to health care and differences in the quality of care Black people receive when they do seek services. In some cases, African Americans avoid seeking services until they are in dire need because of the experiences they have had engaging with culturally incompetent doctors.

A significant amount of risk comes with being Black or African American in the United States. Living under a pandemic only makes the situation worse. There is an old saying in the Black community that if America catches a cold, the Black community gets pneumonia. If we want to take an honest look at why Black or African American people experience so many challenges in this country, we must talk about racism. To truly talk about racism, let us take a high-level walk through the timeline of the Black experience in this country.

2

Background on the Black Experience in the United States

Before we jump into the details, there are a couple of things I want to note for clarity. First, here and in the rest of this book, I will be using the word "Black" instead of saying "Black or African American." While both terms are acceptable, many people have a personal opinion on which identifier feels correct. As a member of the community myself, I most align with the term "Black" to describe my identity. I realize you may have questions about that, and we will explore identity, skin tone, and language a bit further in the book. For now, I want to make sure it is clear when I say "Black" from here on out, it can be exchanged for "African American."

Second, I am not a historian, but I am a Black woman and have been engaging in the inclusion and diversity space for a couple of decades. The information I am going to share is historically accurate but not all-encompassing. My intention is to share a summary of events that will serve as a frame of reference for why Black people experience the United States the way we do today. American history, of which Black history is a part, is incredibly layered and unbelievably interesting. Should you find your curiosity piqued by any of the details shared here, I encourage you to dig into them further at your leisure. You will find an unbelievable set of stories that will capture your interest for a very long time.

Let's jump in.

History of the Black Experience

The Black experience in America began when Blacks arrived in the American colony of Jamestown, Virginia, as enslaved Africans in 1619. As you can see by the timeline shown in Figure 2.1, slavery spanned a time period of 246 years until 1865, which is when the Civil War ended.

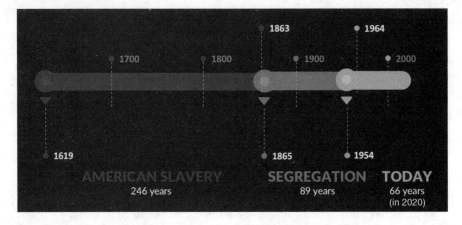

Figure 2.1: Timeline of Black people's existence in the United States of America

Beginning in 1865, Black people were segregated from White people in the nation as it went through a period of Reconstruction—slaves were freed and attempts were made to move the Confederate states (those that had seceded) back into the Union. Reconstruction, which is a rather kind name for a very troubling time, continued until 1877. After Reconstruction, the segregation of Black people continued until 1954, when the US Supreme Court corrected its sanctioning of legal segregation with *Brown v. Board of Education*. The ruling stated that racial segregation in public schools was unconstitutional. This landmark decision was the beginning of the end of segregation, and we entered the period we are in today.

This timeline gives a good visual representation of the injustice Black people have experienced this country, but for context, let's zoom in a bit more.

Segregation

Close to the end of the American slavery period, there is the date 1863. In 1863, President Abraham Lincoln issued the Emancipation Proclamation, which many people believe to be the end of slavery in the United States. The Emancipation Proclamation did declare that slaves were free, but as with most of history, it wasn't quite that simple. The Emancipation Proclamation was passed while America was still engaged in the Civil War, which started in 1861. It was passed because

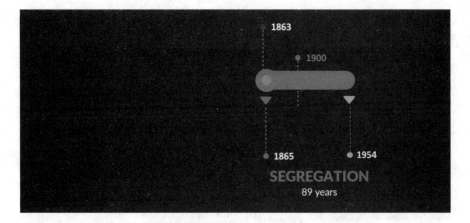

Figure 2.2: Timeline of Black people's existence in the United States of America between 1863 and 1954

the North was losing the war and needed additional troops. Thus, the proclamation allowed the North to recruit from the class of enslaved Black men. The Emancipation Proclamation said that slaves were free in the Confederate states of South Carolina, Mississippi, Florida, Alabama, Georgia, Louisiana, Texas, Virginia, Arkansas, and North Carolina. At this time, these Confederate states were at war and even had a separate president—a man named Jefferson Davis. How enforceable do you think the Emancipation Proclamation was at that time?

In addition to the Confederate states, there were slaves in other states that were still a part of the Union. These states, known as border states, included Maryland, Delaware, West Virginia, Kentucky, and Missouri. The Emancipation Proclamation did not address slavery in the border states, only those in the Confederacy. In a further twist of irony, because the Confederate States of America had its own president, the Emancipation Proclamation was freeing people it didn't really have governance over.

The Civil War went on for another two years until April 1865, when General Robert E. Lee surrendered. After his surrender, the last slaves in the Confederacy in Galveston, Texas, were notified on June 19, 1865, that they were made free by Abraham Lincoln's issuance of the Emancipation Proclamation two years prior. Black people celebrate this date as a holiday known as Juneteenth. In fact, many Black people elect to celebrate Juneteenth instead of July 4th, which is American Independence Day, because Black people were still enslaved in 1776 when the Declaration of Independence was adopted. Juneteenth is gaining more popularity over the years as it has it been brought into the mainstream.

It's important to note, though, that there were still slaves in some of the border states even after 1865. In fact, slavery wasn't legally abolished until the passing of the 13th Amendment to the United States Constitution, which was submitted in 1864 and ratified in 1865.

Complicated, right?

So essentially, all Black people were not "legally" free in all of America until 1865 as a result of the 13th Amendment.

There is also the complication of the language in the 13th Amendment. The verbiage says, "Neither slavery nor involuntary servitude, except as a punishment for crime whereof the party shall have been duly convicted, shall exist within the United States, or any place subject to their jurisdiction." Read that again. No slavery or involuntary servitude is permitted *except as* a punishment for a crime that someone has been convicted for committing. Imagine being newly freed in a nation that has profited off of free labor. Imagine there is a loophole—being convicted of a crime—that can send you back into involuntary servitude.

Black Code laws, which began at the end of the Civil War, created the opportunity for Black people to be forced back into servitude. These laws were designed to limit the freedoms of Black people and to ensure the availability of labor for those who still relied on slavery. States would require Black people to sign labor contracts. If they refused, they were committing a crime. Other Black Code laws included not being permitted to drink from a White man's well, not being permitted to reside in the limits of the town except in regular service of a White person or a former owner, not being permitted to be out past 10 p.m., and even charging Black people $2 a day for days they did not labor to be paid to their employer. Talk about no days off! In this case, days off cost Black people actual money, and if they couldn't pay, they had to work it off.

At the end of the Civil War, many Black people had no choice but to labor for new or former owners because they had no place to go once they were freed. Black Code laws made it hard for Black people to migrate without risking being forced back into servitude. Two forms of Black Codes were pig laws (named because pigs were often stolen) and convict leasing. These types of Black Codes sent Black people to prison labor camps for breaking trivial laws, and their labor was often "leased" or "sold" to White contractors for cheap labor.

Over time, Black Code laws transitioned into Jim Crow laws, which were similar in that they governed the behavior and movement of Black people. The name "Jim Crow" originated as a minstrel show character who was dressed in rags and was played by a White man in Blackface. Blackface is when a person (typically someone who is not Black) paints their face with black makeup to portray a stereotype of or mock Black people. Jim Crow laws included banning interracial marriage, making it a crime for a Black man to light a White woman's cigarette, requiring that restaurants serve White patrons or Black patrons exclusively, and requiring separate seating and entrances to theaters and opera houses for Whites and Blacks.

Lynchings were a common occurrence during segregation. Lynching happens all over the globe, but in America, a lynching is an execution and torture that occurs outside of a trial, typically by a mob of White people to punish or intimidate Black people. Lynching a Black person became a popular form of punishment during the Reconstruction period, and it was most often done by hanging or burning a person alive as a spectacle. According to the NAACP's website, from 1862 to 1968, 72.7% of recorded lynchings were of Black people. In the same period, 27.3% of lynchings were of White people being lynched for helping Black people or for being anti-lynching. A quick Google image search of lynching in America returns hundreds of images of hanged Black bodies surrounded by smiling White people. How important has lynching been to America? Well, the first anti-lynching legislation was introduced in 1918 by Leonidas Dyer. It was not until February 26, 2020, that an anti-lynching act, known as the Emmett Till Anti-Lynching Act, passed in the House and is still sitting in the Senate. Yes, you read that right, and it is not a typo. Lynching is still not outlawed in 2020.

I want to paint a full picture, so it is important that I share that some Black neighborhoods were formed and very successful during the period of segregation. In these areas, known as Freedom Colonies, Black people were able to both survive and thrive without being subject to the Jim Crow laws and lynchings they would be exposed to in other parts of the nation. One such well-known community was the Greenwood District in Tulsa, Oklahoma. Greenwood was a thriving community of Black-owned businesses including law offices, grocery stores, and hotels. Due to the harsh Jim Crow laws in Oklahoma, Black people's cash flow largely stayed in the community, leading it to be known as Negro Wall Street or, in modern terms, Black Wall Street. Unfortunately, Greenwood was destroyed during the Tulsa Race Massacre of 1921.

There are a great many more details and stories about segregation. Segregation was by no means a sense of true liberation for Black people despite what the laws suggested. The years that follow the Civil War were rife with problems for Black people, even though they were legally free.

Today

Figure 2.3 shows the start of the post-segregation era beginning in 1954. So, what happened? How did segregation come to an end?

Well, the change started in schools. Segregation meant that Black children went to school with Black children and were taught by Black teachers while White children went to White schools with White children and White teachers. This also meant that public schools, mostly funded by local tax dollars, created a caste system where more resources poured into predominately White schools. In 1954 the US Supreme Court established that racial segregation in public schools was unconstitutional via the landmark case *Brown v. Board of Education*. Sixty-eight years prior, *Plessy v. Ferguson*, another US Supreme Court case, had upheld segregation and allowed for schools to be "separate but equal."

The *Brown v. Board of Education* 1954 ruling was met with resistance from both Black and White people, but it is this US Supreme Court decision to desegregate schools that began the Civil Rights Era and transitions us to the post-segregation period on our timeline in Figure 2.3.

Figure 2.3: Timeline of Black people's existence in the United States of America between 1954 and today

Segregation did not stop in an instant. Just take a stroll through a few neighborhoods and you will see that de facto segregation (segregation that is not sanctioned by law) is still alive today as a result of the de jure segregation (segregation that is based on law) that has taken place over the years. In fact, it wasn't until 10 years later, in 1964, that the Civil Rights Act of 1964 was passed, which put a legal end to segregation. Essentially, a full decade after schools were legally desegregated, the Civil Rights Act of 1964 was passed, outlawing discrimination based on race, color, religion, sex, or national origin. The act also prohibits unequal application of voter registration requirements as well as racial segregation in schools, employment, and public accommodations.

Let's pause for a moment here and consider a few things.

- From 1954 when *Brown v. Board of Education* desegregated schools to 2020 is 66 years.
- The Civil Rights act passed in 1964, which means for essentially 56 years, Black people have been free from slavery and segregation.

My father is in his 70s. We have well-recognized leaders of large corporations in their 70s. Many of the most powerful political leaders in the United States are in their 70s or older. Consider what that means for the experience of Black people in this country for a moment. Consider the mindsets that people might have if they lived through segregation in this country and are alive and making decisions today.

Black people have essentially had 56 years to make a life for themselves in this country. As history has shown us, mindsets don't change just because laws change. So if we consider the thought process and potential bias of people in their 70s making decisions today as teachers, lawmakers, and leaders in their workplaces, what might we expect to see? How might these mindsets impact how people lead? Well let's take a look at the modern-day experience for Black people in this country, because we see evidence of the impact of oppressive mindsets every day:

- The media describes Black people protesting as rioters or looters, but White people as protesters or scavengers.
- When we hear about White people moving into a neighborhood, it is "up and coming," but when Black people move in it is "going down."

- There is coded language to describe Black people or neighbor-hoods, like "urban" or "ghetto."
- There is an idea that Black people are lazy, although these are the descendants of the same people who were used for hundreds of years for labor, building many famous buildings in the United States, including the White House and the US Capitol. Also, the vast majority of Black, poor people work every day.
- Discrimination shows up in technology—facial recognition software has problems with accurately seeing and identifying people with Brown complexions.
- Until very recently, bandages, crayons, and even makeup were challenges to find in almost any shade of brown.

These issues might seem minor, but if you are not a Black person, put yourself in the shoes of experiencing a life designed by people who are not like you who have the power and influence to shape how you experience freedom. It complicates life in some of the simplest ways: A run in your stockings before a big interview can't be solved with a quick stop at the pharmacy. That expensive new phone you bought that unlocks with your face doesn't work well on your skin tone. When you go to the new neighborhood grocery store, families around you lock their car doors as you pass.

When we hear the term "civil rights," it conjures black-and-white images of marches, speeches by Martin Luther King Jr., and messages from Malcolm X. The Civil Rights movement started in the 1940s and picked up momentum after World War II. Rosa Parks was the secretary of the Montgomery Chapter of the NAACP in the 1940s. We tend to imagine these events as being a very long time ago, but they weren't. The Montgomery Bus Boycott, a notable event during the Civil Rights era, began just 65 years ago in December of 1955. Malcolm X was killed in 1965, the year after the Civil Rights Act of 1964 was signed into law. Martin Luther King Jr. was killed in 1968, just before the passing of the Fair Housing Act of 1968. Many cities had race riots in 1967 and 1968. The post–Civil Rights period has been riddled with battles for equity:

- Fights against systemic oppression
- Concerns with the mass incarceration of Black people through unfair application of laws

- Hate crimes like burning of Black businesses, homes, and churches by White Nationalist groups like the Ku Klux Klan
- Red lining, where Black people were purposefully denied access to services by the government and the private sector involving everything from credit cards to home loans
- Racial profiling and police brutality

The stories of these offenses have been told for decades through music, art, and marches. Today's protests are not new or even much different from the press for racial justice and equal rights in the 1960s. Today's demands to stop police brutality and vigilante justice are no different from the cries for kindness from Rodney King in 1992, the outcry over Travon Martin in 2012, the "What happened to Sandra Bland?" queries in 2015, and the ongoing calls for the arrests of the cops who killed Breonna Taylor in March of 2020. The names of the people who have been lost or brutally injured are many—men, women, and children.

So, when people ask, "How did racial inequity become such a big problem?" and "Why are these protests happening now?" The answer is, we didn't just get here. This experience has been centuries in the making. What happened to George Floyd was not unusual or unique to Black people. It was not a few bad officers or a misunderstanding. It is the consequence of a prejudiced and racist system that has gone unchecked for centuries, and people are fed up. George Floyd was the most current tipping point, right in the middle of a pandemic, because there was nothing else on television. There were no sports, there were no celebrity updates. The only thing on the media's mind, except the coronavirus, was the slow killing of a Black man who lay in handcuffs on the ground saying he could not breathe and pleading for his life while an officer had his knee on his neck.

We're hearing about people marching, we're hearing about Black Lives Matter, which I'm going to touch on in a moment. We're hearing all of these things and it's from a people who have been oppressed for what amounts to over 400 years in this country. Two-hundred forty-six years of being enslaved, 89 years of segregation, and, most recently, 66 years where we are still under systemic oppression, experiencing hate crimes, White Nationalism and the KKK, housing discrimination—all of these things still happen in the United States today. So when you're thinking about the past and what is still happening that we have covered in the timeline and ask, "Why are all these people out protesting? What happened? What made this occur?" it's because people are tired of being oppressed both by law and by the circumstances created by the laws of old. Black people have been carrying around the history of mistreatment for a very long time, and we've been tiptoeing around it. In some cases we've been working for decades to be seen and treated equitably as well as to push conversations about our continued mistreatment and oppression into the mainstream.

PROTESTS WE'RE SEEING TODAY ARE THE RESULT OF 400 YRS. OF OPPRESSION

BLM

If this historical context is new to you, this information is a lot. It might feel shocking or you might even feel some guilt. That is normal. Remember, this is emotional work. This is work about lives and safety and livelihood. This is awareness. You do not have the option of being colorblind anymore. Black people have never had that opportunity. You see us and you see color. Your focus can't be about wanting Black people to see you differently or to know you are one of the "good" people, no matter your identity. If you want to be an ally or an advocate or even more, your focus, from here on out, should be on two things:

- Changing how you see Black people
- Changing how you see yourself in the work of antiracism and racial justice

This work isn't effective if it is just about being liked and feeling good. That isn't motivation enough. Black people have learned to make others comfortable in order to protect their own safety. If you are White or White appearing, the reminder that allyship isn't comfortable or about you being seen as "good" pertains doubly to you. This work isn't always going to feel good, but if you decide to do it, it will feel just, and just is what you are working for as an ally.

After walking through the historical context and the current landscape, it is important that, whatever discomfort you are feeling, you sit with it for a moment. I want you to feel that because your colleagues, your friends, people who are allies, Black people who are walking around in their skin—they feel it all the time. Then sometimes what happens is they feel that feeling and someone says, "Well, all lives matter."

So, let's talk about all lives matter.

When a person says "All lives matter," what it sounds like to someone who feels that feeling we had walking through that timeline is that the way things are is okay. "All lives matter" discounts all of the challenges that Black people have experienced. In reality, no one is saying that all lives don't matter. They do matter, but "All lives matter" is an ideal because it has not been the case. "All lives matter" in response to "Black lives matter" comes across as a counterargument. It sounds like you're saying the status quo is okay when the status quo doesn't work for everybody. Ideally it should. However, here in reality, for Black lives to matter, there have had to be US Supreme Court cases and amendments passed to grant civil rights. No one is ever saying that White lives or any other lives don't matter. It's important to understand that when you hear "Black lives matter," the message is not only Black lives matter. The message is Black lives matter too.

It is of note that Black folks are not the only people who have and are impacted by racist policies and injustice in this country. Many people of various backgrounds who have come to call America home feel the sting of racism while living in the United States. Specifically, though, Native Americans, the population of people indigenous to this country, have faced discrimination, harassment, murders, and theft of their land starting over 120 years before the first enslaved Africans arrived in America in 1619. Although I focus on Black people in these opening chapters, it is important to know that discrimination and oppression affects more than just Black people, and the skills, tactics, and ideas presented in this book will help you learn to be an ally and an advocate for any marginalized group.

Questions to Consider

1. Did this history present new information to you? What did you learn?
2. How do you feel about Black Lives Matter after reading this history? Did it change any perspectives for you?
3. What ways do you see de facto segregation in your day-to-day life?

Research the following if you want to learn more:

1. What Black Code Laws or Jim Crow Laws existed in your home state?
2. What is sharecropping? How did it come about?
3. Who was Emmett Till? What happened to him? What is the most recent news about this case?
4. What was Seneca Village? Where was it?

3

Allyship and Advocacy

Allyship and advocacy are not new terms, but in the current climate we have been hearing more and more of these words. People who are coming to awareness about the troubled history of Black people and other marginalized groups are curious about what they can do to move toward a more egalitarian experience for everyone. Allyship and advocacy are essential brave behaviors to help change the narrative, but not everyone is clear on what these terms mean for their own behavior. Allyship and advocacy go beyond social media posts and starting book clubs but focuses on learning how to engage and connect to people different than you are so you are able to personally identify how you can support them.

What Is Allyship?

Allyship is when someone with privilege and power seeks to learn about the experiences of a marginalized group of people, develops empathy for them and identifies ways to extend their own privilege to the marginalized group. Allies are identified by their ability to apply what they have learned about a group of people because they find ways to transfer the benefits of their privilege to those who lack it. Allyship requires taking the time to become invested in and have emotional connection to marginalized people who are different from you. The part to zoom in on here is the labor part of allyship. An ally seeks to learn about—allies do the labor of understanding so they can connect and build empathy. To be an ally, you have work to do, and most of that work is on yourself. Ally is not a title; it is a verb.

Since protests for racial injustice began in spring 2020, people have been hearing calls for allyship from those impacted most by systemic and systematic oppression. In response, many have donned the title of ally. You might have even read the definition and said to yourself, "That's me—I am an ally." But seeking to understand so you know how to apply your privilege requires a series of actions on your part to ensure that, although you believe you are an ally, others around you would consider you an ally. Remember: Being an ally is not a title you can wear; it is a label earned by what you do. How will you know you are an ally? People will tell you! It will show up in sentences like "Amber has been a great ally for me by . . ."

Allyship is not just for Black people. In light of the current movement against racial injustice, I've made a point to share insight on the history of Black people. However, you can use the skills of allyship and advocacy to support Lesbian, Gay, Bisexual, Transsexual, Queer (LGBTQ), Disabled, Indigenous, or any marginalized or underrepresented group of people. Let's discuss the six behaviors you can practice that will earn you the opportunity to be considered an ally.

Behaviors of an Ally

In the pages that follow, we explore six categories of behaviors that someone seeking to be an ally should put into practice. Since allyship is a verb and requires action, in this section, we cover the many actions that help allies learn, establish connection, and build credibility.

ALLYSHIP BEHAVIORS

1. Expect to be uncomfortable.
2. Make space for imperfection.
3. Seek and expect feedback.
4. Speak up and give feedback.
5. Be an attentive listener.
6. Exercise empathy.

Expect to Be Uncomfortable

I have said this a few times but it bears repeating: Equity, inclusion, and diversity work is emotional. We can see ourselves in the work and at times take things personally. Seeking to learn about a marginalized person's experience comes with a lot of feelings, curiosity, and difficult-to-digest information. You are going to feel a lot. You are going to be tired. You are going to be frustrated. All of these emotions are normal.

Much of the information we learn about those we are seeking to be allies with has been considered impolite to talk about: privilege, racism, homophobia, police brutality—all of these until very recently were considered impolite topics of conversation in the workplace and in mixed company. When we are thinking about being an ally, though, acknowledging that there will be discomfort and knowing how to move past it is incredibly important. There are some tactics you can use to help you manage the discomfort that arises so you can move past it.

First, **practice identifying for yourself the feelings that bubble up**. It's so important that you recognize, "Oh my gosh, I am so emotional. What is this feeling?" Then define the emotion, because once you can define it, you can start to think about why you feel that way, and that can help you to shift your perspective. Discomfort for me usually starts in the pit of my stomach, and I know to ask myself as it bubbles up, "What triggered this?" Usually once I can identify it, I am able to move past it or ask for more information. One of the students in my class once noticed he was uncomfortable whenever he heard the term "White privilege," so he asked, "Can you explain why it has to be White privilege and not just privilege?" Once I shared why we say "White privilege" in some contexts (which I explain later in this book), he was able to move past the trigger and lean into the lesson.

Second, **remind yourself that change causes discomfort** and learning to be an ally and to discuss inclusion and diversity topics confidently is a change. Even good change can be uncomfortable for a time. Imagine you purchase your dream home; the moving process, no matter how you approach it, is uncomfortable. After some time settling in and, well, finally finding the box you packed your underwear in, the discomfort subsides. A bit of the discomfort of doing the work of allyship does subside if you give it time.

We go through lots of changes. We're never the same after them, but we learn to adapt. Everything is always evolving, and social equity work is no exception. Looking for the end-all, be-all solution isn't the right approach. Being an ally is a lifestyle change. While protests across the globe have begun to subside and our social media feeds have started slowly going back to "normal," systemic racism is still very much alive. Homophobia is still very much alive. Sexism is still very much alive.

Expect that change is always on the menu when doing the work of confronting discriminatory systems.

This leads me to my last tip to help you manage your discomfort: **Do not personalize**. This is easier said than done, I know. Much like my student who felt uncomfortable with "White privilege" because he is White, you are going to hear terminology and learn ways you are participating in oppression that will feel like personal attacks. You're going to have conversations that are difficult. It is in those moments that you will be tempted to decide to check out. Don't. We need you. This is not personal. You didn't pick your skin. No one else picked their skin either. We are addressing systemic issues that we are all participants in, whether we mean to be or not.

Make Space for Imperfection

I know firsthand from teaching leaders in organizations about inclusion and diversity that everyone is at a different starting point with how to create inclusive spaces. People are going to make mistakes. *You* are going to make mistakes. Likely you are concerned about that; don't be. Mistakes are going to happen; just accept it. I have been doing this work for 20 years, and I still makes mistakes. Identity is complex, so even the most skilled person is prone to an error that rubs someone the wrong way. Bravely embrace that it will happen.

Before we get into the tactics you can use to make space for imperfection, let's talk about what imperfection is and what imperfection is not.

Imperfection is unintentionally (out of lack of awareness or otherwise) saying or doing something wrong or offensive and being willing to sincerely apologize and correct it when you realize it was wrong. For example, I once had an HR leader on a call say in response to a question about representation of Blacks in the company, "We have always been open to hiring good Black people." Eek. Good Black people? Do you also hire good White people? Why isn't this sentence just "good people" or "Black people" if the intent is to highlight the focus on diversifying the organization. Fortunately, the leader caught himself and immediately apologized. Did everyone forgive him? No. Does he have work to do to shift his own bias? Definitely. But what he said was a mistake, and he was able to realize it was wrong, apologize, and correct it.

In May 2020, a woman was walking her dog, off the leash, in the Ramble in Central Park in New York City. The Ramble is an area where pets are supposed to be leashed because it is intended to be a space for people to observe nature, including birds, which is what a man was doing there when he happened upon the woman with her dog. He asked her to put her dog on the leash, she declined, and the off-camera exchange turned into a recorded encounter where the woman, who is White and standing a couple yards from the man, says to the man, who is Black, "I'm taking a picture and calling the cops," according to the video. She then yells, "I'm going to tell them there's an African American man threatening my life!"

As evidenced by the video, no one threatened this woman's life. She threatened a Black man that she would call the police, intending to scare him, especially by adding she felt her life was threatened. The way she behaved and her choice of words weaponized the fact that she is a White woman and he is a Black man. It also showcased her awareness of what saying that an African American man is threatening her means to a police officer.

You may have heard about this incident in the news. The woman went on to sort of apologize, but mostly to express embarrassment and guilt after losing her job, her dog, and being charged with making a false report.

None of what unfolded in the park that day is imperfection or a mistake. The woman may regret it, she may be embarrassed and even have remorse—but what she did was not imperfect; it was deliberate and malicious.

See the difference?

Making space for imperfection in ourselves and others is a challenge in the current climate. It might seem like one misstep can lead to confrontation and potentially being publicly shamed. I get that, but this is precisely why it is so important to lean into the labor required to create safe spaces. Allies don't act out of deliberate malice. They make mistakes. Here are some tips to help you to navigate your own mistakes and make space for others who may make a misstep.

The number one thing you can do to make space for imperfection is to **build meaningful and trusting relationships** with people who are different from you. Not just passing acquaintances or fleeting connections—actual relationships with depth. Why does this matter? Well, think about the people you are close to now. When you accidentally do something to offend them, does it destroy your relationship? Are you able to discuss what happened, even if it is embarrassing or uncomfortable? How quickly does the relationship recover? Easy water under the bridge, right? Meaningful relationships work that way. When you value a connection, you grant grace for people to learn and grow. They grant you grace for the same reason. Meaningful connections create safe learning spaces.

Meaningful connections also help you identify flaws in your own thinking so you can resolve your own imperfections. Once I was moderating a session about racial injustice and invited people to share their stories. A well-respected and deeply loved executive, a Black man, told a story about driving on a Saturday afternoon in his luxury late-model car. The police pulled up behind him and followed him for a few miles. The officer even followed him through the winding streets of his neighborhood. The leader eventually pulled into his driveway and opened the garage door. The police officer was now sitting at the end of his driveway. As the man got out of his car, he raised his hands and called out, "Hey, what is going on?" He was scared. The officer rolled down his window, was very apologetic, and drove away. When the leader shared this story of what he assumed was racial profiling, the entire room took a deep breath. People teared up. We had to take a break so people could compose themselves. The idea that a police officer would do something to someone they cared so much about was disturbing. It also helped people to see a situation differently because it involved a person they cared about.

Another way to make space for imperfection is to **practice using candor**. Say what you mean. If you mean "Black" or "African American" people, don't say diverse. If you mean White people, don't say "non-Black." Say the words you mean. I know you are sensitive to this language and I can take a few guesses on why, but if you can't say what you mean, we can't have a meaningful conversation about how to address the problems. Using the correct terms helps people understand what you mean. In the event something is incorrect, they can address it with you and you can learn. We are used to softening our language. We say "people of color" when we mean "Black" or we say "I was discriminated against because I am a woman" instead of "I encountered sexism." When we dress up our language, it leaves room for misunderstandings and reduces our opportunities to connect, learn, and grow.

That leads me to the next tactic that makes space for imperfection: **See vulnerability as a strength**. Being willing to share our own learnings, wins, and flaws helps others to see the humanity in us. In my training sessions and throughout this book, I share a lot about my own mistakes. I tell you stories of things I have seen and ways I have experienced favor and discrimination. I want you to understand how important and powerful vulnerability is and to illustrate that I offer it at every turn. When you are vulnerable with someone, you invite them to get to know you a bit better and connect to your humanity. Remember: These issues, the things we are looking to push back against, are *human* issues. So, seeing the humanity in one another is critical to being a great ally.

I don't get it right all the time. I have been doing this work for decades and I still need people to make space for me to be imperfect. I am going to say and do things wrong; it is part of the work. Here's a story: I have a friend I adore and who is an incredible human being. She is Singaporean. And when I initially met her, it was over the phone. She saw a training I did and reached out to connect so I talked to her briefly on the phone and we built a relationship over work email. She sent me an invitation for dinner the next time I was in town. From her emails, I knew her last name was Wong. In my brain I decided, "Oh, she's probably a White woman married to an Asian man." Why do you think I did that? What was I basing that assumption on? If you guessed her accent, you are right. She had what my ears heard as an American and even Southern accent. So I go to meet her for dinner for the first time. I arrive a little late, and I'm looking for White woman, and here is this short Asian woman who walks up to me and goes, "Hi, Amber," because she knew exactly who I was. I was embarrassed. I am pretty sure I even told her that her English was remarkable. Cringe-worthy, I know. Guess what though? She has been one of my dearest friends since that meal. We have built a meaningful and trusting relationship where she learns from me and I learn from her. We lean bravely into our vulnerability, and it's made our friendship incredibly strong. We rely on each other to be candid in ways that help us both grow.

The last tactic for making space for imperfection is **remind yourself that everyone is on a different part of the journey**. You are going to see people who are just coming to awareness about what racism is or what allyship means. As you learn more, you are going to see a lot of almost accurate but not quite right information online. Your job is not to correct everyone and everything. My job is not to correct everyone and everything. Everyone is trying to figure out how to lean into this work. What we have to do is continue to encourage curiosity and have meaningful conversations so people can continue to progress on the journey to allyship.

This work will exhaust you if you see it as your responsibility to correct every single thing you see that isn't quite right all over the world. Instead, focus on your learning and the learning of those close to you—your friends and family. You can make the most significant impact as an ally and an advocate by speaking with the people with whom you have established relationships, credibility, and influence. It takes bravery and may be uncomfortable, but that is a part of allyship. You should start there.

When you encounter a behavior that you are compelled to correct that falls outside of those close to you, the first thing to do is to ask yourself "Is what this person said or did harmful?" Will someone's safety, identity, or physical person be harmed if you do not speak up? If the answer is no, then let it go. Everyone is learning. You hear someone say Latino instead of Latinx? Let it go. They may be still learning terminology. It is not harmful. You notice someone referring to the large bedroom in a house as the master bedroom and you know that terminology comes from American slavery? Let it go—again, people are still learning. When it comes to very minor things that do not cause harm but may not be technically correct, give people the grace you want for yourself when it comes to learning. Now, if it is harmful or puts someone's life or safety at risk, you definitely should speak up. Later on in this section I share tactics for how to speak up without laying blame or being seen as confrontational.

A point of note here because "woke" culture is real and is very much alive and well online. Woke culture is the idea that you are a part of the "elite" group of people who are "aware" of something—in this case, how to be an ally or being antiracist (a term we discuss in Chapter 5). Social media and woke culture will make it easy to feel like you know a lot about how to be an ally or how to be inclusive. Sometimes this will lead you to critique or lecture others. Here is a word of caution: Diversity, equity, and inclusion work is ever evolving, and you will never, ever know all of it. No one is perfect. If all you have is critique, you should turn your critiques inward. Take a long look in your own mirror and critique yourself. How can you improve? Where are you not showing up authentically? What ways are you not being brave? What makes you feel like you need to shame or embarrass people? Ask yourself the hard questions and address the areas where you can improve. I promise if you focus on your own flaws, you will find it a lot easier to be less critical of others who are learning because it will be clear we all have work to do.

Seek and Expect Feedback

With imperfection comes the opportunity to learn. One of the best ways to learn is to seek and expect feedback. We may never know what we are doing wrong or what we are doing well if we are not intentional about seeking feedback. Seeking feedback isn't necessarily easy, though, because feedback is a bit of a mixed bag. Feedback can be awesome or it can be terrible, which can cause us to be uncomfortable with the idea of intentionally seeking it. Here is the thing, though—the more you train yourself to seek and expect feedback, the easier it is to hear both the good and the bad and not have it be emotionally unsettling. The more you seek feedback, the more you build your fortitude.

So, how do you seek feedback? Well, the best way is to **ask** others around you for it! Often people may have feedback for us, but because much of our culture in America teaches us to be kind, people will not volunteer unless you ask. If you really want to know how you are doing or how your messaging comes across or if you are being equitable, ask. Make sure that you ask in a thoughtful way so people will tell you the truth. For example, if you are a leader and you ask your whole team to "give me your feedback" in a meeting, likely you will not get very much. No one wants to critique their leader in front of others and risk damaging their own self-image or brand. However, you can ask people individually and in safe and private settings to share their thoughts with you. Will they tell you? Maybe and maybe not, but asking is a great first step. Even if someone does not have any feedback to share, you asking in a responsible way lets them know you are open to feedback. If they have some to share at another time, they are more likely to come to you.

One point of note about asking for feedback in the current climate: We're in a very interesting place right now where people are confronting racial injustice very openly. As we covered when we walked through the timeline in Chapter 1, people are feeling the pressure to push for change. You may be getting a lot of messages, especially if you're on social media, about not asking Black people questions. And I want to make sure I clarify: If you are asking how you did on something, if you are asking for insight on your behavior, and if you create an environment where people feel safe sharing that with you, that's ideal, that's seeking and expecting feedback, and it is okay. However, it is still a possibility that you may be met with resistance from Black people. Remember, no one owes you feedback. Sometime people are feeling a lot of pressure and just don't have the capacity to engage in feedback at all. That's okay. Give people space to not be ready to engage. Keep in mind that when you invite feedback, you should be open to the possibility that some people cannot give any.

Some feedback that we receive we won't like, but allies recognize when it is necessary, even when it doesn't feel great. Very early in my consulting career, I did not have staff yet and I did a lot of traveling, so I often took introductory calls in the airport. I asked a woman I had done some work for and with whom I was building a relationship to share whatever feedback she had on her experience working with me and with Cabral Co. She *loved* the services I provided, which was awesome. She also said, "Listen, you were incredible. You give a great training. The team connected with you and leadership is very happy. But you should never take another call in the airport." I froze and said, "Wow, really? Can you tell me why?" She proceeded to tell me, "The experience I had talking to you in the airport did not even come close to the experience I had talking to you when you were not busy traveling. When you were able to focus, the conversations were so good and the training was totally worth the investment." Tough feedback, but so valuable. I tell her to this day I am so grateful that she felt comfortable letting me know her experience. For me it was a perfect reminder to invite feedback as often as possible because you will be able to identify the behaviors and habits that can cause others to feel excluded or judged.

Sometimes feedback is tough and our instinct is to immediately challenge it. Instead of challenging the feedback, consider: **If this were true, how would I respond to it?** Don't focus so much on if you think uncomfortable feedback is true or not. In the scenario above, I didn't push back on the client giving me feedback, although I wanted to say: "I don't have any other time to take phone calls." Instead I considered, What if it is true that my airport meetings are not going well? What would I say to that if it is true? Having that mindset made it easier for me to hear what she was sharing with me as a possibility. As a result, I ultimately saw the feedback as useful and made a change in managing new client calls. Put this question in your pocket for use when you catch yourself wanting to push back on someone: "If this were true, how would I respond?" At times we can't see past ourselves, so it is possible that a better question for you is "If this were my daughter telling me this, how would I respond?" Feel free to replace "daughter" with your favorite person in the world. How would you want them to experience your reply?

You have probably heard that feedback is a gift, even when we don't like the feedback. What do we say when someone gives us a gift, even if we don't like it? Thank you. Always say thank you and **be appreciative of feedback** that people share with you, even if you are not sure you are going to use it. Saying thank you lets people know you appreciate the feedback and also appreciate whatever emotional obstacles they may have had to overcome to share the feedback with you. No one owes you feedback, and there may be times when people will decline to give feedback. So when you do get it, express gratitude.

When you are receiving feedback from someone, **avoid being reactive**. Sometimes this is hard, because receiving critique can set us on the defensive. We are inclined to explain what we meant and how we intended to message this or that. Your reaction can stifle someone sharing feedback with you, either good or bad. I encourage you to assess if you are even ready for feedback. When someone approaches to share their thoughts with you—even if they jump right into what they have to share—if you feel frustration building, stop the person from continuing. Say something like "Pardon me for interrupting, I appreciate you for coming to me with feedback. I am not yet in a place where I am ready to listen. Can we set up some time to discuss this later?" This tactic allows you to prepare yourself for the conversation, which makes it a lot easier to set our personal emotions aside and listen. It also keeps you from messaging defensively in the moment.

Be careful with this tactic, though. If you tell a person that you want to take some time before receiving feedback, make sure to follow up and set up the talk time. In the short term, you might feel tempted to let the moment pass, not follow up to hear the feedback for fear it is negative. If you fail to follow up, though, you are messaging to others that you are not open to feedback. As we covered earlier, feedback is one of the ways we learn how we are doing, so if no one wants to give you feedback, you are missing out. Also, you are inadvertently messaging "I don't care what you have to say" to others, and they may choose not to share valuable information in the future and even may let others know you are not receptive. Allyship requires that we learn about others so we can develop empathy for them, and learning through receiving feedback is a part of that process.

While you are preparing yourself for feedback, consider a few things that can help you to give balance to your emotions:

- Feedback I receive may not be bad; it could be good!
- Feedback is an opportunity for me to learn.
- Feedback gives me a chance to notice trends in my own behavior so I can identify natural skills and weaknesses.
- Feedback isn't an indication of who I am, it is an indication of something I did that I can do differently or something I did well and should continue.

Be mindful about getting preoccupied with your intended message and working to clarify what you meant. Ultimately, what matters is your impact. Receiving feedback from others is a critical way to get to the heart of the impact and impression you actually made on others. It will allow you to adjust your behavior to be able to move closer to making the impact you intend in the future.

Let's imagine you get your emotions together and sit down with someone who has feedback for you, and the feedback is tough. You learn that you said a few things that were offensive to some people. While you didn't intend to do harm, it is clear your words or behaviors have caused some to be excluded or disrespected. You come to the decision that it is important you **apologize** to start making things right. Apologies are a critical life skill, because as I have shared, we are all going to make mistakes. I encourage clients to carry the spirit of apology. "Carrying the spirit of apology" means having the keen awareness that you might make an error and that apologies are an essential step toward recovering from our mistakes. We all should know how to deliver a robust and meaningful apology.

What does an apology sound like? An apology includes two parts:

1. I apologize for _____.
2. Moving forward I will _____.

I apologize for mispronouncing your name. Moving forward I will make sure to say it correctly.

I am a heterosexual woman with short hair. People often assume I am a lesbian—I am guessing because of my hair and because I am not often in dresses or skirts. I always correct people, but I would appreciate hearing "I apologize for assuming you are a lesbian. Moving forward I will practice not assuming things about people's identities."

An apology is not conditional. It is not "I'm sorry you feel that way" or "I didn't mean to offend you."

Using the above examples, saying "Oh, I have a friend whose name is spelled the same and she says it differently," or "Oh, my bad, I thought you were a lesbian because of your haircut," is not an apology. Those are justifications. When you have done something wrong or offended someone, people aren't interested in your reasons, people are interested in you apologizing and saying what you will do in the future. It isn't about you and how you feel; it is about you recognizing you made a mistake and taking ownership of it.

There is a lot to be said about apologies, so I make a point to embed how to deliver effective apologies in every lesson I teach to my clients. Also, as powerful as good apologies are, they are often done very poorly. Companies apologize badly for racist products and advertisements. Public figures apologize poorly for discriminatory remarks and, almost always, folks slip right into "We didn't intend to offend" defensive language. Who cares if you didn't mean to do something wrong? You did do it, so apologize. When someone crosses a line with you, their personal reasons seldom carry any weight if they cannot clearly and meaningfully apologize. Practice it if you must: "I apologize for this. Moving forward I will do that."

Apologies are a big part of allyship, and as such, in later chapters of this book, we speak a bit more about them, including some of the concerns that women have with apologizing and what to do if you are not sure what the right behavior should be after offending someone. We also cover how to decide if you should be apologizing or if there is another behavior you should lean into instead.

Today, there is a mad dash for many to learn how to be a "good person" and be seen as an ally. This has caused a lot of White and White-adjacent people to ask their nearest dearest Black or Brown friend to help them understand "if this sounds racist" or if "people will be offended by" something. I know we are all learning, but don't rely on anyone to be a spokesperson. No one can speak for everyone in a marginalized group. This applies for all marginalized people. There is no one gay person who speaks for all gays, no disabled person who speaks for everyone with a disability, no White woman who speaks for all

White women. **Do not rely on someone to be a spokesperson** based on an aspect of their identity.

NOTE   "White-adjacent people" are people who appear to be White and benefit from appearing White although they may belong to another racial or ethnic group.

So, what do you do when you want to know if the term to use is "Black or African American"? What do you say when you want to make sure you are not offending members of the disability community by using the word "disabled" instead of "differently abled"? You can ask someone you feel comfortable asking with whom you have built a strong relationship. It might be a friend who belongs to a particular group. The problem isn't the question, it is believing that the answer someone gives you to your question applies to *all* Black people or *all* disabled people or *all* members of the disability community. Aside from a few blatantly discriminatory exceptions, whatever answer you receive is true for that individual person. You should therefore internalize the information as "My friend prefers to be called Black" instead of "I should say Black people instead of African American people." I know. It probably feels like you are going to say something wrong that way. You are going to call someone Black who wants to be called African American, and you really don't want to offend anyone.

Guess what? There is no magic bullet to safely refer to all members of a particular group. There's no one name or term that all will find acceptable. You have to be willing to stand corrected should how you address someone not resonate. You have to get to know people on an individual basis, learn folk's individual preferences, and go from there—just as you want to be done for you.

Another point on treating individuals as spokespeople: Not everyone is equipped to discuss the nuances of equity work. Just because people are of a certain identity doesn't mean that they can explain entirely what that means. All Black people are not going to be well versed in American Black history and be able to explain in detail the reason for the Black Lives Matter movement. Every White person does not have a working knowledge of the Ku Klux Klan. When you want to learn, lean on people who are visible and credible experts in the space. Pay attention to the resources they share, the way they speak, and the lessons they teach. Take control of your own learning and protect your personal relationships by learning from teachers instead of members of the community. Otherwise what feels like questions to guide your learning to you can feel burdensome to the person you care about, even if your intent isn't malicious.

Speak Up and Give Feedback

Receiving feedback is only half of the feedback loop; true allies also speak up and give feedback to others. Most of us are better at giving feedback than we are at receiving it. That is, until it's time to be brave and discuss the topics we normally avoid talking about. Then we get nervous, are unsure what to say, and sometimes are crippled with fear of saying the wrong thing. When you are working to be an ally, speaking up and giving feedback to others is how you cultivate a culture of candor and accountability. You should view giving feedback respectfully and responsibly as a way to ensure everyone is doing their best to create a culture of belonging.

Speaking up and giving feedback starts with you **saying something when you see or hear something that is inappropriate**, especially if it is in a space you engage in frequently, such as with friends, family, or in the workplace. It didn't happen to you? It doesn't matter. Allies speak up. How do you speak up? Well, it depends. Sometimes you may be in a situation where subtlety is best. Let's explore an example.

Maybe you are in a large meeting or in a public place, so you don't want to be disruptive but feel that something needs to be said. I remember being in a meeting once where we were discussing the talent on the team because we wanted to hire for a new manager. We were considering whether the role should be posted internally only or both internally and externally. I suggested a star performer on the team as a possible internal candidate, and a peer said, "Well, you know, she doesn't come across professional." My instincts told me the peer was reacting to the star performer's dark skin and her always evolving (and always neat) hairstyles but instead of speaking on my assumptions, I simply turned on my curious demeanor and asked, "Hmm. Can you help me understand what you mean?" The peer looked at me a little embarrassed and said, "Well, she is very talented. You're right, she really could be a good person for the role." The encounter wasn't confrontational at all, but by asking my colleague a question, she caught her own bias and corrected herself.

Some other ways to challenge in an indirect way are by saying "Hmm. I am not sure I follow what you mean" or, my personal favorite, "Can you say more about that?" Remember to pour on the curiosity when you ask; this keeps the encounter from going from a slight nudge to seeming confrontational or an attempt to embarrass someone. Our frustration sometimes makes us want to embarrass the person, but if the goal is to get people to be different, embarrassment is not a useful learning tool. Consider how you feel when you are embarrassed. Embarrassment can lead to confrontation, which is disruptive to learning.

There are going to be times that call for a more direct sentiment. When you hear or see something that is clearly wrong and will do harm to another person's reputation or identity, you should speak up, even if you do not think the speaker meant it. It might be uncomfortable, but you have to push past the discomfort and remember that allies understand that sometimes they are the only ones who can safely speak up, even if they have to push past their own discomfort. Let's consider what speaking up directly might look like.

Stephanie has worked for the government most of her career and has a very high security clearance, allowing her routine access to sensitive information to do her job. Six months ago, looking to broaden her skill set, Stephanie made a shift to working in the public sector leading a team of ten. The public sector is notably more diverse than her previous roles. You notice in meetings that Stephanie mixes up her direct reports and often mispronounces their names. After one meeting, you mention to Stephanie, "You almost rolled the wrong person off the project in there. We really need Ramesh, but I agree Adita might excel elsewhere." Stephanie rolls her eyes and says, "I'm sorry. I mean, I used to work in a high security area and over there I worked with people named Jim and Mary, not Ramesh or Adita."

This example is not a subtle nudge situation. This is a situation where Stephanie can do great harm to people by mixing team members up, even terminating the wrong person's job. Stephanie is also casually demeaning people by calling them the wrong names. She feels justified in calling people the wrong names because they are not names she is "used to" like White-sounding names such as Jim or Mary. Stephanie has been in her role for six months and is still mixing up the names and identities of people who report directly to her. Stephanie's behavior is harmful and needs to be addressed directly.

What do you say? "Stephanie, I find what you said inappropriate and offensive, and I'd like to share why. When is a good time for us to touch base and discuss?" You can make this statement even more specific: "Stephanie, I find your remark about Ramesh and Adita's names inappropriate and offensive, and I'd like to share why. Let's find some time for a touch base to discuss." An alternative approach is to say directly to Stephanie what the correct behavior is, but doing this requires that you know exactly what the issue is and can speak to it immediately. I would say something like "Stephanie, I know you strive to be an inclusive leader, so it is not optional to learn the names and identities of the people who work for you. Your comment about Ramesh and Adita's names is racist. It suggests that you are not willing to respect the ethnicity of diverse people because their names are unfamiliar, but you will respect someone named Jim."

Is this hard? If you are new to allyship, I can imagine it might be. Speaking up is one of the ally behaviors that takes consistent practice and bravery. The more you do it, the easier it becomes to spot when something isn't right and to actually say something about it. Some other ways to speak up directly include simply calling it out with a sentiment like "That remark is racist. Let me tell you why." Or consider asking a question: "I think you mean well, Stephanie, but the comment you made comparing Jim and Mary to Ramesh and Adita sounds racist. Is that you meant?"

We discussed earlier how we might not always be ready for feedback. Well, that's true for those we want to give feedback to as well. The person you want to give feedback to might not be ready! When possible, **ask for permission to share feedback** instead of blurting your thoughts out to someone. If we are going to share some perspective with someone, we want them to be in the best space to receive it, whether the message is good or bad. Asking for time to discuss allows the person you want to speak to the opportunity to emotionally prepare for the discussion; it is a way of communicating respect.

I do a lot of facilitation, and I know the hour or so right after I teach a class is not a good time for me to receive feedback. During that time I am usually replaying the session in my mind, making notes about the things that went well, and kicking myself for the parts that I forgot to include. I find it best for me when the client I am supporting says to me after a session, "I would like to share some feedback from the session with you. Can you let me know when there is a good time?" It allows me the opportunity to be in the right place to hear the value in the feedback. Of course, immediately after an experience, most people's instinct is to share their thoughts, but next time, consider asking "Hey, I would like to share some feedback. What is the best way for me to share it with you?" You may find someone wants feedback in the moment, which is great! If they don't, though, you are setting them and yourself up for success by establishing a time that works well for both of you.

Speaking up and giving feedback also means **advocating for those who are not in the room**. "Advocating for someone" means openly supporting or calling attention to a perspective or cause. Advocating is not speaking for someone or being someone's voice. Remember, we are all individuals, so it is not possible for one person to speak for someone else. However, we can advocate to make sure diverse identities and perspectives are being heard. Being an advocate means noticing when a group of Americans are planning an event that will have attendees from around the world and speaking up to say: "I notice we are all American but this event will include people from around the world. Can we make sure we include some planners who have a global lens?" Advocating is about pointing out what perspectives are possibly being overlooked so experiences can be more equitable and inclusive. Advocating might sound like saying "I am not sure we are being thoughtful about members of the disability community in this decision." Another example: "I notice we are all heterosexual, White women. Perhaps we should consider including the perspective of our affinity groups in our planning." At times, including additional perspectives may feel like it can create delays, but, remember, if you don't make time to do things right from the outset, you will have to make time to either do it over or, worse, risk public criticism. In the last several months, you may have noticed many companies being very transparent about the lack of diversity in their leadership or on their corporate boards. Many of these organizations are publicly recognizing the mistake in not having diverse representation and are working to change that. If you approach interactions with others, especially in spaces where big decisions are made, with an advocate mindset, you can help avoid being in situations where poor representation is a concern.

Last, when speaking up and giving feedback, be aware of and **use your own power and privilege**. Sometimes you will find that you have the ability to influence decisions, impact others behavior, and help educate others simply by virtue of your identity or position. As a

Black woman, likely I have a certain degree of power and influence when speaking with another Black woman. The same is true for your identity. There is a certain unspoken sense of trust that exists with people we share identity with; use that trust. If I see another Black woman in need of assistance or who could use some feedback, I am willing to step in. I understand that the connection we have as a result of shared identity makes her more likely to hear what I have to say. This works across many layers of identity: people with disabilities, people who are gay, people who are immigrants. We discuss more about privilege in Chapter 11 so you gain a better sense of what it means to have privilege and how to use it to be an ally and an advocate for others.

Be an Attentive Listener

A lot of us think we are really great listeners, but what we really are good at is listening for directives. Being a good and attentive listener means you go beyond listening for what you can do or what the solution is. It means you recognize the value of hearing people's stories and understanding how people feel. By being attentive listeners, allies can connect to the people they are looking to understand and support.

When someone who is part of an underrepresented group is sharing something with you, **pay attention to their verbal and nonverbal messages**. We speak with our mouths but also hands, our eyes, and sometimes even our whole bodies! We are messaging all the time. A good listener is paying attention to all of that in addition to listening to the words. As a young person I used to walk around my granny's house with earphones—partly because she didn't want to hear the kind of music I was listening to at the time. She'd sneak up on me and scare me because I couldn't see or hear her coming. After she was done laughing, she would always say, "Listen with your whole body, Amber." When I am hearing someone who is passionate or sharing an important message, I remind myself to listen with my whole body. I pay attention to what I am sensing and experiencing as well as to what their body language may be communicating. These days people spend a lot of time not saying exactly what they mean but alluding to it. If you pay attention to those cues when you are listening, you will start to be able to discern anger from frustration, happiness from gratefulness, and many other subtle expressions that people reveal when they want to be heard. You can also use this skill to sense when you have offended someone or if something isn't quite right.

Another key to being an attentive listener is **creating a safe space to have dialogue**. By "safe," I mean that a person will feel confident that they can speak freely and not be judged, attacked, or demeaned and that the discussion will remain confidential. We don't always do the best job at creating a safe and private environment for discussions unless we see the conversation as private. One of the keys to creating a safe place for candid dialogue is intentionally considering the possibility that the person you are looking to connect with needs safety and privacy. As you are learning to be an ally and building relationships with those different from you, create opportunities for people to feel comfortable sharing. This can be as simple as asking if someone is willing to share their thoughts with you and making sure that you are able to listen without distraction.

Sometimes people new to allyship are so eager for everyone to see and know the challenges of the marginalized people they are learning about that they unintentionally put people on display by asking them to share personal stories or perspectives in meetings or explain to people what steps they can take to support their community. This is not candid dialogue, and it does not make people feel safe. As you are learning to be a good ally, it is important that you are focused on your learning and doing your part to listen. If you think something might be good for others to hear, ask yourself first, "Would I want to talk about this in front of others?" If the answer is no, then don't ask someone else to share. If the answer is yes, then ask the person you are connecting with if they would be willing to share. Be sure to ask in a way that makes it clear that "no" is an option. An appropriate ask for someone who is responsible about safe space might be: "This story is very powerful and I think others need to hear it. I also understand we are speaking in confidence and you might not want to share, and I will respect that. Would you be willing to talk about this openly?" Listen with your whole body to their response to your question. If their words say yes but their nonverbal behaviors say no, listen to the nonverbals. At times people in marginalized groups feel pressure to comply even if they aren't comfortable doing so. Good allies can sense when they may be creating an environment that a person will not feel comfortable in.

When you are listening to those you are serving as an ally for, make sure to **listen to understand and not to respond**. You may have heard the Epictetus quote: "We have two ears and one mouth so that we can listen twice as much as we speak." We learn through experience that listening is about taking action and looking for the problem we should solve. When it comes to building connections with marginalized groups, listening has to be about learning. Hearing the stories of Indigenous people, Black women, or whomever you are interested in being an ally for is one way you can develop empathy and a connection to the experiences of that group of people. If you position yourself as a learner, you have the opportunity to identify ways in which you may experience life differently and to see clues to how you might be able to serve as an ally. Remind yourself that you aren't looking for an action or directive when you are listening to understand; you are focused on learning.

When we are listening to others, sometimes we hear things we do not agree with, so we might be inclined to assert our perspective, as we would in any other passing conversation. When learning about the experiences of a marginalized person, we should **be confident listeners**. Most of us are really confident sharing our stories and drawing connections or challenging ideas that don't resonate with us. Since so much of being an ally is about hearing about someone else's experiences that are sure to be different from our own, we should practice listening as confidently as we would ordinarily share. Confident listening is quiet, pays attention to what is being shared, and gives cues to the speaker that you are paying attention. I often recommend people practice being confident listeners when the person sharing their experience is very passionate. Confident listeners don't personalize or critique; they understand that the speaker's passion is not an attack on them. Confident listeners stay out of debates and ask insightful questions rather than questions that may diminish or invalidate someone's experiences. We have all had the experience of trying to share something with someone who seems consumed with sharing their own perspective. It can leave us feeling unheard. In some cases, we may decide not to have another discussion with that person. Being a confident listener takes practice because we are so used to sharing our experiences to let people know we understand. Confident listeners can sense when it is time to just listen and acknowledge rather than share personal stories of their own.

The last skill of an attentive listener is to **be mindful of redirection**. Redirection is when someone is sharing something that might be sensitive or takes some bravery to share and another person tacks on their idea onto the end of it, causing the sensitive topic to go unacknowledged. For example, imagine you are planning a team offsite meeting that involves a day full of physical activities. You realize that there are a couple of team members who are not very active and another who just returned from maternity leave. During your next meeting with the planning committee, you say, "I think we are not being mindful of everyone's skill sets and needs by having so many physical activities." Just as you finish your statement, another team member chimes in: "Yeah, and I think the shirts we selected should be in different colors so people can break out into teams." The rest of the committee leans into the last comment, leaving your concern about the level of physical activity for the day unacknowledged. That is redirection. It can happen to anyone, and it may or may not be intentional. What redirection does is it signals to people that you don't really want to hear what they have to say. For people who are part of marginalized groups, who often do not feel seen or heard in general, redirection can cause them to disengage and choose not to speak up again. Redirection is sneaky, easy to miss, and also easy to ignore when it happens.

When you do witness a redirection, make a point to circle back to the first comment. You can say something like "I heard you say something about the level of activity we are planning for the team offsite. Can you share more?" It's a simple and courteous way to make sure people know they are heard, and it encourages them to continue speaking up. If you are on the receiving end of a redirect, I don't recommend choosing to opt out of future communication. I recommend speaking up again, but this time framing it as a question that people feel compelled to react to. Using the previous example, you could say, "I have a concern about our plans for the day. Is this the right time to share?" Saying no to that question is pretty rude, so it is unlikely anyone will do so. This approach also ensures that you will be heard when you raise the matter again.

Exercise Empathy

Empathy is such an important part of allyship, it is even part of how we defined allyship in this book! "Empathy" means you are aware of and are sensitive to the feelings or experiences of others. It means that you are able to put yourself in someone else's shoes and relate to the emotions they are feeling. "Empathy" means you understand someone else's experience and the impact it is having on their life. When expressing empathy, we have to be careful with what we mean by "understanding."

At times, telling someone that we understand can come across dismissive of their circumstances, especially when we are speaking about aspects of identity. When showing empathy, our approach should be "I understand this experience is challenging," or "I understand this is hard to manage." Understanding should not be comparative, such as "I know how you feel. I felt the same way when _____ happened to me." While we can understand, we can't really ever know how someone is feeling, so we want to be careful. Also, empathy is not about comparison but sharing, so we should try to avoid comparing someone's experience with our own. Empathy is also not the same as pity. Pity is feeling sorry for someone's misfortune or regretful that they are suffering. In allyship, pity is an off-putting emotion. Marginalized people want your empathy, your ability to see and acknowledge their situation such that it moves you to action. Pity can make people feel looked down upon, when many marginalized people are very proud of their identities even when they are exhausted by oppression. We treat people differently when we empathize with them; it makes us handle people with care and intention.

One way allies can exercise empathy is by checking in and reaching out to people when something is happening in their communities. For example, many people felt compelled to check in on their Black friends when the video of George Floyd's murder was publicized. When you empathize with someone, you express care by seeing how they might be feeling under challenging circumstances. Checking in should be done responsibly and with careful language. Some ideal phrases to use when checking in on someone you care about are:

- *I will never pretend to know how you feel, but I am here if you want to chat.*

  This sentiment acknowledges that you know something hard has happened, without assuming you know how someone is feeling.
- *I see you. I hear you. I support you.*

  These statements work well independently or together. They are best used when someone has shared that they are having a challenging time or when you can see by their behavior that they are struggling with something.
- *Please let me know what you need from me.*

  This statement puts you in the situation of supporter for someone who is having a hard time. Sometimes the answer will be "I don't need anything," and that is okay. There is no need to be pushy.

■ *What can I do to emotionally hold space for you?*

This statement lets people know you are aware there are emotions involved and that you grant them space to share those emotions. Again, people may choose not to share, but the sentiment goes a long way.

There are some things to keep in mind around exercising empathy. It is possible you are not a part of the Black community and are feeling the magnitude of the moment. Perhaps you are even coming to awareness about ways in which you have treated Black people or other marginalized groups unfairly. All of these are good growing pains. They should not incite you to reach out to people you do not have an active relationship with. Don't call your Black roommate from ten years ago to check on her and apologize about what is going on. If you don't have a relationship with someone, your desire to check in is more about you than it is about them. Although you may have a general concern about how they are doing, what you are really feeling is guilt or responsibility, and you are checking in to see if they feel negatively toward you. Consider for a moment: Someone you haven't talked to in a decade or more reaches out to see how you are doing because they heard your grandmother passed on. They happen to have met your grandmother once in a passing encounter. It will feel a little strange for this person to check in on you, right? You also might not have the emotional bandwidth to deal with connecting with someone from long ago while you are grieving the loss of someone you cared about. You may even be skeptical about the reason for their check-in. Check-ins are for people you know and care about, not for people with whom you no longer interact. If you find yourself feeling a genuine urge to check on someone from long ago, do so at another time when things are not so heavy.

There are also some statements you should avoid when checking in on someone, especially someone you know but don't have a deep personal relationship with. Here are a few of them:

■ Are you okay?
■ Just checking in.
■ How are you holding up?
■ Do you need anything?

- Can you tell me what to do?
- How can I help?

Each of these statements is a bit too casual to feel meaningful to the recipient. I realize sometimes your intention is to come across gently, but think about how it might land on the receiver of the message. Making a more intentional statement has greater impact. Now, of course, if you have a well-established close relationship with someone, these light touches might work just fine.

The last two statements on the list are especially concerning because they make the assumption that you are not a part of the problem. It is very possible that you have or are behaving in a way that is challenging or not helpful. Instead of these statements, a better approach is to ask: "Would it be helpful if I _____?" This allows a person who may be under emotional pressure to reply yes or no instead of them having to find a solution for you.

Empathy is all about feeling. So when you are exercising empathy, you should **allow space for emotions to surface**. Anticipate that if you are exercising your empathy around an event, it's possible for people to become unexpectedly emotional. In the weeks following the killing of Breonna Taylor, an EMT in Kentucky who was killed by police when they entered her home looking for someone they already had in custody, my emotions came in waves and often unexpectedly. In the middle of a virtual training session for a client, I teared up and found myself emotional. When a community is dealing with a loss or a specific and potentially fresh injustice, emotions can be raw and running high. Set your expectations for unexpected emotions to arise and allow room for them in your discussions. Many people consider emotions a private matter, so when someone shares their feelings with you, consider it a sign of trust building, which is essential for an ally.

The year 2020 has been full of bold and public statements about equity, social and racial justice, and dismantling oppression from people and organizations alike. White people have been protesting with the Black Lives Matter movement and taking stands against racism. For those of us on the receiving end of these behaviors, it is all a little jarring. Suddenly, routine trips to the mailbox have been met with a car full of White people yelling "Black Lives Matter" as they drive past. The behaviors are new, and some of the encounters feel strange to Black people who have never encountered so many friendly White people.

That said, if you are White and new to allyship, **expect some resistance and skepticism**. A few weeks ago, my colleague, a very tall, dark-skinned Black man, rode his bike to the local grocery store, as he has done for many years. On this trip he made it to self-checkout and realized he left his wallet at home. As he is fumbling with the keypad to see if he can pay with Apple Pay, another customer, a White woman, walks up to him and says, "Do you need some help?" He replies, "I'm okay, I was just looking to see how to pay with Apple Pay." He notices the woman doesn't appear to work there so he follows up with "Do you know if they take Apple Pay?" The woman turns around, asks a nearby clerk, and they learn the store only takes Android Pay. As my friend begins to gather his purchases to take them back to the shelves, the woman pipes up, "I can buy it for you." My friend freezes. All of his internal alarms are going off because never in his 30+ years of life has a random White person ever been so kind. He says, "No, thank you. I can come back. It's okay." The woman pushes: "It's okay. I don't mind! It's like $12 worth of stuff, I can get it." They go back and forth for a moment and, out of fear he is causing a scene, he allows her to pay for the groceries. He asks her for her Venmo or CashApp; she declines. She paid for the groceries and told him to have a nice day. My friend still feels a little strange about this. He isn't sure if he handled it well or if he should prepare for more random acts of kindness from White people who seemed to ignore his existence altogether before the killing of George Floyd. I share this story with you to say, when you change your behavior, it may alarm some people. That is okay. If you mean it, continue on. Just be aware that people may have some reservations about your behavior.

***

The steps we have gone through explain the work of being an ally. These steps are also the same behaviors you need to exhibit to have a growth mindset. A "growth mindset" means you believe that your basic characteristics can be cultivated through application and experience. It is the idea that you can evolve, learn, and improve through your own effort. A growth mindset is the ideal lens through which to approach social equity because it encourages the openness necessary to inviting growth. Having a growth mindset also helps allies to engage in conversations around identity, life experiences, and interpersonal differences respectfully. As you hone the skills we have covered in this chapter, you will find that people will look to you to be an ally, they will come to value your insight and openness, and they will trust that you have their best interests at heart.

Advocacy

Advocacy is the process where someone with privilege and power is willing to take steps to protect, publicly support, and dismantle systems against a marginalized group of people. In order to be an advocate, you have to be willing to do additional work beyond getting familiar with the nuances of marginalized groups and developing empathy for them. It is about taking action to change how others experience the world. Similar to allyship, advocacy is not a title, it is a verb. There are actions that you have to take to be considered an advocate.

Sometimes people mistakenly believe allyship is less important than advocacy. That is not true. Both roles are necessary. A simple way to distinguish between the two is to recognize that allyship is focused on the individual and their unique experiences and perspectives. Advocacy is focused on the systems. In order to be an advocate, you have to protect people from harm, you have to publicly support people having access and being heard, and you have to be willing to dismantle systems that may serve you but are not equitable for others. To be an advocate, you must be willing to do all of the things we discussed under allyship but add one additional step: Take personal risk. It is the willingness to take personal risk that sometimes leads those in activism circles to use "accomplice" rather than "advocate." Advocate or accomplice behavior means being willing to take risks to push for equitable treatment.

Take Personal Risk

Personal risk is the critical difference between being an ally and being an advocate. While allyship does require that you advocate for people not in the room, being an advocate means you are willing to put yourself at risk to protect, publicly support, or dismantle systems against a marginalized group. Putting yourself at risk can look a lot of different ways so let's discuss the tactics around putting yourself at personal risk.

An advocate **shows solidarity**. "Solidarity" means showing support with your actions. It is one thing to agree with someone; it is much more impactful to agree with someone and accompany them in the process of protecting, advocating, or dismantling. People who show solidarity are unafraid of being seen expressing their support and are willing to openly challenge the status quo. Solidarity can be as simple as asking tough questions or as audacious as participating in a protest, strike, or walk-out. Being in solidarity means "I am so committed to your cause, I will stand with you although I may not be personally affected."

Taking personal risk also requires you **use your power and privilege** to make others feel seen and safe. I have a very close friend who is a transwoman. I work to be an ally to all womxn and am especially passionate about safety for transwomen who are Black. I know that Black transwomen are being harassed and even murdered so I pay attention to my friend while we are out. When she leaves the group to go to the bar, I am watching. If she leaves the group to go to the restroom, I usually go to the restroom too. I don't ask her if she wants me to go with her. I don't tell her to let me know when she is going to the restroom or bar or anything. I want her to feel agency in the decisions she makes, and she doesn't need my permission to live her life. In fact, I don't even know if she notices that I go to the restroom at the same time she does. Her knowing really isn't the point. As an advocate for transwomen, I see it as my responsibility to make sure she feels safe. I have heard horror stories of transwomen being confronted and even attacked in restrooms. So, I go. If something happens, I will be there to intervene. So far, thankfully, our trips to the restroom have been uneventful.

NOTE   Make a mental note of that "x" in place of the "e" in womxn; we discuss it in Chapter 5.

It is nothing for me to go to a public restroom. I never worry about being confronted or feeling unsafe at all. That is a privilege. It sounds unreal, but there are people who are afraid to go to a public restroom. If you don't worry about using the restroom, you too have privilege.

We discussed being an **advocate for others** under the allyship section, but when it comes to advocating for others in the role of an advocate, there is a little more to it. Remember, advocating for someone means openly supporting or calling attention to a perspective or cause. When you are serving as an advocate, it is more than just ensuring that people are considered and invited to participate. Advocating for others in the role of an advocate willing to take personal risk means you will create space and opportunity for others to feel safe, seen, and heard. It is the difference between saying "Hey, I notice we need some different perspective" and "I have the mic, but I would like to invite someone else up to speak instead of me." Advocating in the role of an advocate means creating opportunities for underrepresented people to speak for themselves about their challenges. It means advocating for changes that will help remove obstacles and systems that are not equitable.

Advocates **fight against systemic and systematic oppression** by dismantling systems that perpetuate discriminatory and inequitable practices, even when those practices benefit them. We discuss in detail what the words "system," "systemic," and "systematic" mean in Chapter 12, but there are many present-day examples of fighting back against systemic and systematic oppression. The many protests against social and racial injustice are an example of fighting against systemic and systematic oppression. An advocate may attend and participate in protests or contribute to organizations that support protests. Advocates also look at the practices of their employers and publicly ask for changes that make the process equitable. Advocates encourage their employers to offer health benefits to spouses of employees, regardless of their gender. These actions are about addressing the systems that perpetuate discrimination, which is what makes them advocacy behaviors and not just allyship.

The last tactic of an advocate is to **operate with bravery**. "Bravery" means committing to protect, advocate for, or dismantle systems even when you are uncomfortable. Being willing to take personal risk requires bravery. Acts of bravery as an advocate can show up in a number of ways. In the workplace, it means being willing to go to bat to ensure talent on your team gets the promotions or resources they need and deserve. In your home, it means being willing to push back against antiquated or discriminatory ideas in your family and with your friend groups. In the world, it might mean joining the layer of White people who physically place themselves between police and Black protestors. Acts of bravery means being willing to be courageous and endure danger to protect, advocate for, and dismantle dysfunctional systems.

Pitfall: Performative Allyship and Advocacy

Performative allyship and advocacy is when someone with power and privilege professes support and solidarity with a marginalized group publicly in a way that isn't helpful, is not backed up with meaningful actions, or actively harms that group. One way to determine if allyship or advocacy is performative is to see whether there is some sort of "reward" involved. The reward might be accolades for a job well done, or lots of visibility, or likes on social media. Performative actions are dangerous because they give the appearance of improvement—we have a committee, a newsletter, a few more Brown faces on our social media posts, for example—but there is no real impact. True allyship and advocacy take a lot of self-work. The work is not neat and easy to capture. It is brave, it speaks up, it asks tough questions, and it can be noisy.

One way you can stay out of performative allyship is to ask yourself three questions:

1. What impact will my action have?
2. Am I able to see, own, and explain my personal responsibility in this system?
3. Is my action about me feeling good or being seen as good?

If it is a social media post, what impact will that action make? Is it about likes and being seen as doing or being good? If the action is you deciding to stop supporting an establishment that has discriminated against disabled patrons, what impact are you having? Can you see your own complicity in oppressive systems? This question will be easier to answer after we get through Chapters 12 and 13, but until then, it is important to realize that allies and advocates understand they are complicit and can explain why and make decisions to behave differently as a result of their complicity.

We have covered a lot in this part of the book. I realize it may be a bit much to consume in text, and I know different people learn differently. It may be useful to revisit the graphic image at the start of Part I. You should be able to follow the timeline and recall some of your learnings. Also, for ease of reference, I've included a list of the tips we have covered for being an ally and an advocate. I recommend picking a few of these to practice for a while so you can start to develop habits around the behaviors. By doing so, they will become a part of who you are. Take a look at the list and pick two that you want to focus on. It's helpful to let those around you know that you are working on them so they can support and share their observations on how you are doing.

ALLYSHIP

- ☐ Expect to Be Uncomfortable
    - ☐ Practice identifying for yourself feelings that bubble up.
    - ☐ Remind yourself that change can cause discomfort.
    - ☐ Manage your emotions.
- ☐ Make Space for Imperfection
    - ☐ Build meaningful, trusting relationships.
    - ☐ Practice using candor.
    - ☐ See vulnerability as a strength.
    - ☐ Recognize that everyone is on a different part of the journey.
- ☐ Seek and Expect Feedback
    - ☐ Invite feedback.
    - ☐ Consider "If this were true, how would I respond?"
    - ☐ Be appreciative of feedback.
    - ☐ Avoid being reactive.
    - ☐ Be prepared to apologize.
    - ☐ Do not rely on anyone as a spokesperson.
- ☐ Speak Up and Give Feedback
    - ☐ When you see something out of line, say something.
    - ☐ Ask for permission.
    - ☐ Advocate for those not in the room.
    - ☐ Use your power/privilege.
- ☐ Be an Attentive Listener
    - ☐ Pay attention to verbal and nonverbal messages.
    - ☐ Create safe spaces for discussion.
    - ☐ Listen to understand, not respond.
    - ☐ Be mindful of redirection.
    - ☐ Be as confident listening as you are sharing; avoid debates.

☐ Exercise Empathy

    ☐ Check in and reach out.

    ☐ Allow space for emotion.

    ☐ Commit to improvement and act.

    ☐ Expect resistance/skepticism.

ADVOCACY

☐ Take Personal Risk

    ☐ Show solidarity.

    ☐ Use your power/privilege to make others feel seen and safe.

    ☐ Advocate for others.

    ☐ Fight against systemic and systematic oppression.

    ☐ Operate with bravery.

Language

I thought it was important to dedicate a good amount of this book to language. A lot of words and terms connected to inclusion and equity work are thrown around, and it is easy to be confused, to use words improperly, to avoid certain words, and even to use the wrong words for things. As the first chapters of this book may have even introduced some terms to you that are new, we will use the next few chapters to explore language.

First, what is language? "Language," according to the *Oxford Dictionary*, is defined as:

1. *The method of human communication, either spoken or written, consisting of the use of words in a structured and conventional way.*
2. *A system of communication used by a particular country or community.*

The first definition is likely close to what comes to mind first for most people, but let's focus on the second definition: Language is "a system of communication used by a particular community." When you are around different people, often you speak a different language. You speak differently to your family at home from how you speak in the workplace from when you are speaking with your friends. You speak to your spouse in a specific language and to your parents in yet another. Although you may be speaking in the same language, depending on where you are and with whom you are engaging, your word choice, tone, and sometimes even your energy changes.

People also speak differently within their own ethnic or racial communities than when they are in mixed company. So, as a Black woman, there are words that I will say with my Black friends that I will not use when I am with other friends. When you are invited into a community as a guest, there are words that you should not say because that language belongs to that community, and you are not a part of that community. As an ally, you may come to be an invited guest of many communities, and you will hear people say words to one another that, if you say them, will be received with offense. I am not a lesbian, but I am friends with lesbians who use terms with one another that I will not use because I am not a member of that community. Who says what *matters*. How something is said *matters*.

Language is actually a part of our identity. Language is how we share impact and experience in different settings. It is intercultural. Your language communicates your standpoint in whichever space you are occupying in that moment. A person's identity and position shapes how a message will be received as well as how the message will be sent. For example, you may have been having conversations about social and racial injustice lately. Perhaps you have discussed these things with your children and with your spouse. The meaning you conveyed may have been the same, but the language you use probably differed.

Many of you are learning to be allies and therefore are learning the language of the allyship community. The language used by allies, advocates, activists, and leaders in equity and inclusion like myself belongs to this community. You may find some of the language to be challenging or uncomfortable to say. That makes sense. You are new to this community. You are still learning. The words are new.

Many of the words associated with inclusion and equity work are used commonly in the activism community. Activism is noisy. It doesn't necessarily give us a good feeling, as it conjures up images of protests and falling statues. Activism uses powerful and vigorous language to call for political and social change. Much of the lexicon around racial injustice is activism language, meaning it is bold, aggressive, and sharp. This activism language has made its way into our workplaces, our dinner tables, and our news feeds this year, and many people find it uncomfortable. Some people want to push back and say, "This language doesn't belong here," because it is uncomfortable. However, this is the language we have for bringing about political or social change. So, it is important to get acquainted with the words and gain confidence in using them so we can communicate clearly.

Some of the words feel accusatory and aggressive. Remember, they are intended to get your attention. So terms like "privilege," "racism," "antiracist," and "Whiteness" may rub you the wrong way. Push past that feeling. The words don't feel friendly because the problems they are describing are not nice. The issues are challenging and hard to talk about. There is no way to say these words and sound positive and upbeat. Prepare for the discomfort. Expect the jarring. The words mean what they mean. They refer to human issues of life or death, issues of safety, and issues of being seen. Don't personalize the terms when navigating discussions; my hope is that this book will help you become familiar enough with key terminology that you can focus on what the words actually mean instead of the emotions they evoke.

Welcome to the community. Here we are responsible for managing our emotional responses to history as we learn how to use new words bravely and correctly. The answer is not to avoid the terminology. When we are allies and advocates, we are willing to adapt even through discomfort and fear. Let's start with the basics.

Diversity

Take a look around you and check off whichever of the following things that you see:

bag or sack	laptop
beverage	light switch
book	notebook
cell phone	photo frame
doorknob	television
eyeglasses	wastebasket
ink pen	window

Look at you, spotting the diversity around you! In simple terms, "diversity" is a variety or mix of different people or things. Diversity exists everywhere and can exist in any category. Considering the last activity, you could easily have some diversity in your photo frames or a diverse variety of ink pens in your space. When you are preparing a meal, you have a diverse mix of ingredients.

Imagine you are going to make pizza; you might have dough, sauce, cheese, possibly some kind of protein, and a few veggies as a part of your ingredients. Each of these items has its own taste and can be prepared or used in any number of diverse ways. Each ingredient might even be pretty tasty on its own! That's diversity: a mix of things all existing in the same space.

When we speak about diversity in society or in our workplace, we are usually talking about diversity of people. In this case, diversity is a mix of people with their own beliefs, experiences, identities, ideas, opinions, and styles. Each of us, while we are all people, have our own unique combination of attributes that makes us diverse. Our personal mix. As a result, when a group of people is together, we are certain to find some type of diversity, even when everyone appears to be the same in some way. Yes, it is true; a room full of White men will still have some diversity. Diversity of viewpoints, age, experiences, religion, and even ethnicity can exist in a room where people might appear to be all the same.

Sometimes people question why organizations across the globe are focused on diversifying—after all, diversity can be found everywhere! Many organizations struggle with having a mix for a few specific categories of diversity, such as gender, race and ethnicity, and sexual orientation. There may be a lot of White people working at a company and not many other races or ethnicities. Some places have a good mix of race and ethnicity, but the mix isn't distributed across job levels. For example, there may be a lot of women working for a company, but there are no women above a certain job level. Organizations have begun to take a good look at their diversity makeup in recent years for a few reasons, but one major reason is that there is data that says it affects the bottom line.

According to McKinsey and Company's February 2015 publication *Diversity Matters*, companies in the top quartile for racial and ethnic diversity are 35% more likely to have financial returns above their respective national industry medians. The publication also reports that companies in the top quartile for gender diversity are 15% more likely to have financial returns above their respective national industry medians. Simply put: Diverse companies make more money.

Social pressure also can play a part on organizations making the move to diversify. Marginalized groups, allies, and advocates typically notice when there is a lack of people from underrepresented groups and may begin to ask questions or call for change. In the weeks of protests following George Floyd's killing, several companies made commitments to take actions to diversify their boards and leadership talent, to financially invest in fighting racial injustice, and to educate themselves and their employees on matters of diversity, equity, and inclusion.

Remember, though, diversity is just the existence of differences; it says nothing about how those differences may shape someone's experiences. Organizations are truly working for ways not just to attract a mix of identities but also to make those identities want to stay with the company and to ensure they are treated correctly and have access to opportunities while they are there.

Before we dig into what it takes to treat people well, let's cover identity since allyship and advocacy connect so closely to identity.

Questions to Consider

1. When you use the term "diversity" in work and in life, are you speaking about the mix of identities or about a specific group of people?
2. Are you part of or work for an organization that includes a diverse group of people? How do you think that diversity, or lack thereof, affects your group?

7

Identity and Intersectionality

Gender, age, race, sexual orientation, religion, income, personal style—all of these things are aspects of identity. They are the myriad of attributes that make us who we are. Identity is the combination of characteristics that comprise who we are. There are too many elements to name that can fall under identity, such as physical appearance, parental status, political affiliation, and ethnicity. Following is a chart of some aspects of your own identity:

ability	nationality
age	parental status
class	physical appearance
gender	political affiliation
income status	race
languages spoken	religion
marital status	sex

Identity is a shared experience in that we identify and label people all the time without even thinking about it—tall, small, thin, male, rich, smart, married—but identity also is incredibly personal. There are aspects of your identity that maybe only you know about. Not all aspects of identity are visible, and of those that are, not all assumptions we make about what we see are accurate. We assume what another's gender, income status, race, ethnicity, and more are based on their appearance. Those assumptions are not always correct, but because we project aspects of our identity just by living everyday life, our identity is a shared experience.

Identity is also incredibly private. Your identity is yours. You and you alone know yourself inside and out. You determine what attributes fit and which do not. You determine what name you should be called by or what your personal style will be. You own your identity. There may be aspects of your identity that you love, share, and celebrate and others you are embarrassed by. Identity is deeply personal and yet, simultaneously, widely shared.

One of the biggest mistakes we make with identity is not understanding that just as we get to define our own identity, so does everyone else. We see ourselves as complex, nuanced, and layered, but we tend to look at others and label them as one thing: She is fat. He is tall. They are smart. We don't do a good job of giving people the opportunity to be more than the identity we assign them, even though we want a say in our own identity and we want to be more than just one story. One of the biggest things you can do when encountering new people is to remind yourself that they are more than what you have decided about them in the first few minutes. Just as you are.

The second thing we don't do well regarding identity is to remember that just because we have decided who someone is in our minds, that is not necessarily how they define their identity. Just because someone feels the most important aspect of my identity is being female doesn't mean that is how I prioritize my identity. We have to learn that people know who they are, just as we know who we are. You don't get to decide someone's gender for them. You don't get to decide someone's ethnicity. You don't get to decide someone's personal style. You decide for you and they decide for them. If your expectation is that people call you as you want to be called, then you have to grant that same right to other people. Regardless of your personal perspective, opinions, or curiosity, you should call people how they want to be called and be open to correction when you call someone wrongly.

I have a good friend named Christopher. He introduces himself as Christopher and signs his emails Christopher. Yet people call him Chris all the time. He hates the abbreviation of his name. He knows what he wants to be called. Sure, there are lots of Christophers who don't mind being called Chris, but he *does* mind. If it were your name, you would want people to call you by the name you are comfortable with.

Brief Notes on Gender Identity ━━━━━━━

Calling people what they want to be called naturally extends to gender identity and pronoun use. That said, I am not going to cover pronoun use in depth in this book. Gender is an evolving topic, and I hesitate to outline any parameters here for something so fluid. I do have a few simple rules I can recommend that I live my own life by:

- Call people what they want to be called. Pronouns are varied. Someone could be he, she, they, zir. You do not decide. Your personal beliefs do not control someone else's identity. If you are unsure, either ask, use neutral pronouns, or use none at all.
- Be open to correction. In fact, encourage correction should you call someone by the wrong name or pronoun. When corrected, adjust immediately. If you make a misstep, just fix it and continue your sentence.
- Don't focus on making people wear nametags with their pronouns or list them in emails. I use nametags intermittently—specifically at large events where the audience is likely to be diverse and also when supporting a client who encourages it. I admit that my behavior in this regard is not consistent, for a couple of reasons:

  1. I have been in far too many rooms where everyone in the room has their pronouns on their chest, but they almost all use gender-conforming pronouns! Then there are a couple of people who use nonbinary pronouns, such as "they/them," and everyone is whispering to each other, "Just so you know, that person is a 'they.'" It feels silly, forced, and sort of defeats the point to me.
  2. I don't like the idea of forcing people, either by practice or by social pressure, to share any part of their identity. I personally know too many people who have spent a good amount of time sorting their identities out—some specifically struggled with their gender. Asking people for pronouns can be anxiety inducing for someone using nonbinary pronouns. So instead, I trust that when folks are ready to share, they will correct me if I call them wrongly. I am prepared to adjust my behavior to meet the ask.

I want to introduce you to a couple other words that are often abbreviated so you know what they mean when you hear them:

- *Cis*, short for cis-gendered—someone who personally identifies with the sex they were assigned at birth.
- *Trans*, short for transgendered—someone who does not personally identify with the sex they were assigned at birth.

Using these terms, a short description of my identity would be that I am a heterosexual, cis woman. That sentence in layperson's terms says I am heterosexual, I was born a woman, and I identify as a woman.

As I shared earlier, gender is an evolving topic, which to me is a good thing. It means more people are feeling safe and confident expressing the fullness of their identities. However, since this book is focused on allies and advocates, I recommend you do your own research into gender identity if the topic interests you. There is a lot to read and learn.

What Does the *x* in "Latinx" Mean?

When describing identity, you may notice the letter *x* appearing in certain words. The addition of the *x* is an attempt to be more inclusive. We discuss what inclusion means in Chapter 8, but for now, consider the next examples of use of the letter *x*.

- *Latinx* is intended to be a gender-neutral version of "Latino" and "Latina"; therefore, it includes all people who are of Latin descent.
- *Folx* is an alternative spelling to the word "folks." While "folks" is already gender neutral, sometimes the *x* is used to strategically message inclusion of all people.
- *Womxn*, pronounced the same as "women," is intended to be inclusive of transwomen.
- *Mx.*, pronounced "miks," is intended to be a gender-neutral alternative to "Mr. and Mrs."

Acronyms

Identity has a lot of layers, and we love acronyms to describe aspects of identity and also to describe certain aspects of inclusion and equity work that touch identity. The risk with using acronyms is that you are assuming people know what they mean, which then puts folks on the spot to ask if they don't know the terms. Also, acronyms keep people from saying the important words related to inclusion and equity work. I am going to define some common acronyms so that you know what they mean. However, I recommend that you do not use the words unless you are speaking with someone you know understands or with someone who works in the inclusion and equity space. Part of being an advocate is helping people to feel seen and safe. Saying the word "transexual" or "trans" when speaking about the transexual community is better than saying LGBTQ+ because it helps ensure that a person's identity is seen. The list is not comprehensive but should be helpful if you decide to start doing your own research.

- AAVE (African American Vernacular English): A dialect of English spoken by African American people originating in the enslaved South. African American Vernacular English is also sometimes called AAE, which stands for "African American English," or AAL, which stands for "African American Language."
- ABAR (antibias and antiracist): Typically referring to a learning curriculum for students that challenges bias and racist teachings and perspectives.
- BIPOC (Black, Indigenous, and People of Color): This acronym is intended to ensure that Black and Indigenous identities are specified when referring to people of color.
- BLM (Black Lives Matter): A political and social movement originating among African Americans, emphasizing basic human rights and racial equality for Black people. There is an organization of the same name.
- DEI (diversity, equity, and inclusion): This acronym speaks about the work to ensure there is diverse representation, equitable treatment, and inclusive experiences for all people to move toward a more egalitarian society.
- LGBTQIA (lesbian, gay, bisexual, transexual, queer, intersex, and asexual): This umbrella term focuses on the nonheterosexual, transexual, and gender-nonconforming community as a whole. Sometimes this is shortened to "LGBTQ" or "LGBTQ+."
- POC (people of color): People who are not White.
- WOC (women of color): Women who are not White.

Intersectionality

We have discussed how there are many aspects to identity, as none of us is comprised of just one single attribute that captures the fullness of who we are. As a result of us having many identities, we can be a part of several different groups. For example, Kyle is a White, male, homosexual and a member of the disability community—as well as several other characteristics. "Intersectionality" is about the interconnected nature of identities such as race, class, gender, and sexuality, and how being a part of several disadvantaged or marginalized groups can combine, or intersect, to compound their experiences of discrimination or oppression. The term "intersectionality" was coined by a Black feminist named Kimberlé Williams Crenshaw in 1989.

So, using Kyle, our white, male, homosexual member of the disability community as an example, he is a part of two disadvantaged groups: homosexual people and disabled people. Intersectionality means that Kyle is likely more disadvantaged because his identity places him in two groups than, say, Thomas, who is a white, heterosexual man who is able-bodied and belongs to no disadvantaged groups. I am a Black woman who is heterosexual and able-bodied. The disadvantaged groups I belong to are Black and woman. If I had a disability of some kind, I would belong to three disadvantaged groups. Intersectionality isn't limited to race, sexual orientation, and physical ability; it speaks about the combination of any identity groups that we belong to that may cause us to experience discrimination.

Remember, none of us is just one story. We are each comprised of many attributes that combine to make us who we uniquely are. Some of our attributes are viewed positively and may help us navigate life while others can cause people to view us negatively and create obstacles for us to overcome. In the end, we are all navigating this life together. Keeping in mind that just like us, others are not just one aspect of their identity can help us to extend grace and empathy toward others, especially when we consider the role intersectionality might play in making the lives of some people more difficult.

Questions to Consider

1. What are the most important aspects of your identity to you? What parts of your identity do people easily associate with you? Are the parts of your identity that you most closely align with and the aspects people assign to you the same or different?
2. Do you find it difficult to call people how they want to be called? Why or why not?
3. Does any aspect of your identity fall within a disadvantaged or marginalized group? Can you think of any instances where you have experienced discrimination or difficulties because of it?

8

Inclusion, Bias, and Unconscious Bias

In Chapter 6, we described diversity as a mix of people with their own beliefs, experiences, identities, ideas, opinions, and styles. Diversity can exist just about everywhere. I asked you to imagine a diverse mix of ingredients to prepare a pizza: dough, sauce, cheese, possibly some kind of protein, and a few veggies. Well, if diversity is the mix of ingredients, consider inclusion the work it takes to make the pizza.

"Inclusion" is valuing, supporting, and connecting with people with their own beliefs, experiences, identities, ideas, opinions, and styles. The definition is very similar to that of diversity, but with three important words at the beginning: valuing, supporting, and connecting. Valuing, supporting, and connecting with others takes work. It requires intentional behaviors, mindfulness, and consideration.

Kindness is not inclusion or equity. More than just being nice to someone, inclusion requires you to get to know people, their ideas, and what they need, and listen to their experiences so you can support them, value them, and advocate for them. Sounds a lot like allyship, right? Creating inclusive spaces is labor. It is the rolling of the dough, the chopping of the vegetables, hand grating the cheese, and carefully selecting the protein to put together a meal that tastes great. It is being considerate of the needs of those who will be enjoying the pizza—who is vegan, gluten free, or dairy free? It is making the diversity mix work together for the people who will be enjoying the meal.

Inclusion is not about agreement, comfort, or harmony. There will be times when being inclusive might feel uncomfortable to you. At times you may have to adjust behaviors that might feel very normal and easy for you, because those behaviors are oppressive or exclusive to others. Sometimes I think one of the biggest obstacles to inclusion is the idea that it should feel comfortable. Inclusion is labor so it is not always comfortable. We all know that growth comes from discomfort. Inclusion, allyship, and advocacy all go hand in hand, and at times they mean that we have to take a hard look at the ease in our lives and consider whether marginalized and underrepresented people have access to that ease as well. Inclusion is being brave enough to make adjustments when we discover that they do not.

I know the word "inclusion" has been a pretty popular workplace term for a while now, but it truly touches everything. Inclusion or the lack thereof is a part of your everyday life experience. Let's look at a few headlines from around the globe in 2020 and see if we can spot how they connect to inclusion.

- "The Coronavirus's Xenophobia Problem" (Although the title of the article seems to have been changed to "The Other Problematic Outbreak," this discussion is still pertinent.)[1]

  This article discusses how the story about the coronavirus in various regions is causing some people to experience xenophobia. "Xenophobia" is prejudice or discrimination against someone from another country. Because the virus has been associated with a specific population of East Asian people, in various parts of the world, people who appear to be East Asian are being treated poorly, including harassment, being refused service in restaurants, and even seeing a drop in patrons for their own businesses. Can you identify the connection to inclusion in this article? Who is not being included?

- "In Landmark Case, Supreme Court Rules LGBTQ Workers Are Protected from Job Discrimination"[2]

  This article discusses the Civil Rights Act of 1964, which states that someone cannot be fired from their job on the basis of their "sex." The case argued whether the word "sex" meant just someone's gender or if it included a broader meaning to include all aspects of LGBTQ+ identity. The ruling extended the rights of

---

[1]Yasmeen Serhan and Timothy McLaughlin, "The Other Problematic Outbreak," *The Atlantic*, March 13, 2020, https://www.theatlantic.com/international/archive/2020/03/coronavirus-covid19-xenophobia-racism/607816/

[2]Pete Williams, "In Landmark Case, Supreme Court Rules LGBTQ Workers Are Protected from Job Discrimination," *NBC News*, June 15, 2020, https://www.nbcnews.com/politics/supreme-court/supreme-court-rules-existing-civil-rights-law-protects-gay-lesbian-n1231018

the 1964 Civil Rights Act to include LGBTQ+ people, meaning they can no longer be fired from a job based on their status as an LGBTQ+ person. How was inclusion at play here?

- "Protests Against Racism Struggle to Gain Traction in Italy"[3]
This article discusses how Italian residents with African ancestry expressed concern that the country was missing a golden opportunity to address discrimination. The Italian prime minister stated that inclusive policies are important and that Italy should also be working to confront racism. Can you identify the connection to inclusion in this article? Who is not being included?

The next time you are watching or reading the news, ask yourself, "Who is being included or excluded here?" You may be surprised to discover that almost all the news we consume is connected in some way to someone or some group of people being treated in a way that they deem as not inclusive or a change being made to create a more inclusive experience. Inclusion is a life matter, not just a workplace issue.

Inclusion doesn't mean everyone all the time. At times, varying identities will be highlighted or focused on that are different from your own. That is okay. There will also be times when you are celebrated, highlighted, or acknowledged, and other people may not see themselves in your identity. It is important not to believe that every single circumstance will be tailored around every identity. Valuing, supporting, and connecting means that there is an opportunity for my identity to be seen, there is an opportunity that someone like me may be the leader, or there is an opportunity that me or someone like me might be centered (made the focus) and celebrated.

In exclusive situations, there is a lack of opportunity to be valued, supported, or connected, because there is a lack of diverse representation. For example, imagine an organization gives an award to their best salesperson. Inclusion means that there is enough diverse representation in the sales team that the person who wins the award might carry a myriad of characteristics. Exclusion or a failure of inclusion is if the

[3]Giovanni Legorano, "Protests Against Racism Struggle to Gain Traction in Italy," *The Wall Street Journal*, July 1, 2020, https://www.wsj.com/articles/antiracist-movement-struggles-to-gain-traction-in-italy-11593611869

sales team does not have diverse representation, so the winner of the sales award is likely to be a specific identity.

Inclusion can also be performative or the product of tokenism. Performative inclusion is when the limited diversity available is put on display and celebrated to give the appearance of an inclusive culture. Tokenism is the act of doing something or giving visibility to someone to prevent criticism or give the appearance of inclusion or equity. Asking a Black person to lead a team that is very visible but has no real power or influence is an example of performative inclusion and tokenism. We discuss tokenism again in Chapter 13.

To determine if inclusion is at play, ask yourself a few questions:

- Do you feel welcome?
- Do you feel safe?
- Do you feel connected?
- Do you feel seen?

If the answers for all of these questions are "yes," it is likely that you will experience the valuing, supporting, and connecting related to being included.

Bias and biased behaviors are another obstacle to inclusion. Let's explore what bias is and how it can be an impediment to inclusion.

Bias and Unconscious Bias

Bias is a preference, inclination, or prejudice for or against someone or something. "For or against" means that bias can be in favor of something or opposed to it. Our biases are influenced by our background, cultural environment, and personal experiences. We are influenced by what we watch on television, where we hang out, who we are friends with, what we do for fun, where we work, and pretty much all aspects of our life.

I have a little news here. Bias isn't bad. It is just the way our minds work to help us navigate the world. The human mind takes in 11 million bits of information every second, but we are only consciously aware of 40 to 50 bits. Since your brain cannot consciously process 11 million bits of information, it takes shortcuts. Your mind processes information that you are already familiar with without much effort on your part. The problem is, sometimes those quick processes that we aren't aware of are based on stereotypes and are inaccurate. Take a look at the six types of people below. Make note of what your brain does when you read each of them:

1. Stay-at-home parent
2. CEO
3. Coffee lover
4. Rapper
5. Genius
6. Nurse

You may have noticed that, pretty quickly, your brain created a person in your mind as you read each character. If you are in the United States, it is likely that your stay-at-home parent was a woman, your CEO was a White man, and your rapper was a Black man. It is also possible that you noticed your bias, so you may have changed your characters somewhat in your mind. Maybe you caught on to the point of this exercise and decided that your nurse would be a middle-aged Asian man instead of a woman. Perhaps you changed your CEO to be Black or your stay-at-home parent to be male. If you made any changes, that is good! It shows that when you become aware of the bias in your brain, you can change your perspective and in turn change your behavior or response to that bias.

It is also possible that your life experience manufactured some characters that fell outside of the norms I just suggested. Maybe your CEO is a woman, so you pictured her. Perhaps your husband or son is a nurse, so you imagined him. All of those responses are okay and are rooted in your own bias. Our brains do this identity construction thing to people all the time.

Think of your favorite DJ or radio personality. Most of these people have amazing voices. Do you remember the first time you saw them? You may have said to yourself, "I didn't expect them to be so tall," or whatever the difference was. You may have even had the same experience with a colleague you've worked with remotely when you met them for the first time. The bias in our brains fills in gaps we aren't even aware of.

This filling in of gaps leads us to talk about unconscious bias or implicit bias, which is a bias we are unaware of that happens outside of our control. It's kind of like you making assumptions about what your favorite radio personality looks like. Unconscious bias gets more attention because if we are unaware of our bias, we can act out in ways that are offensive to others and not know about it. In fact, the only way we can learn that we have an unconscious bias is for someone to tell us.

Many of our conscious and unconscious biases are rooted in stereotypes we have about different identities. For this reason, sometimes our biases are inappropriate. Want a few quick examples? What comes to mind when you hear "convicted felon"? What about "protestor"? And "attorney"? How do you treat convicted felons? Protestors? Attorneys? Have you ever considered your actions around these identities before? Martha Stewart is a convicted felon and a beloved retail business woman. The late Martin Luther King Jr. was a protestor and also one of the most recognized Civil Rights leaders of all time. Hillary Clinton and Barack Obama are attorneys.

Let's consider a few examples of bias so you can see what I mean by saying it helps us or can be an obstacle to inclusion. Keep in mind, we can be aware of these biases or not aware of them.

Conformity Bias

Conformity bias is when we take cues from the actions of others rather than exercising our own independent judgment. This is the bias that makes us imitate others. Imagine being new to an organization, eager to put your best foot forward. Conformity bias is how we learn the organization's culture and figure out the unwritten rules. We imitate others. We adopt their language. Some organizations have employees, some have team members, some have associates—we learn the language of the organization by imitating what we hear so we can conform to the standards of that organization.

Conversely, conformity bias can create some obstacles to inclusion. When someone falls outside of the norm, we may say they are not a "culture fit." Conformity bias can cause groupthink and make people feel that challenging the status quo is unacceptable. "Go along to get along" and "This is how we do things here" are phrases you may hear that are rooted in conformity bias.

Similarity Bias

Similarity bias is the tendency to surround ourselves with people who are like us or remind us of ourselves. Similarity bias is cool because it helps us make friends. Think about the people you consider friends. Likely you have quite a bit in common. You may have even picked up new friends as you took interest in new things. Runners tend to attract other runners. If you are a parent, you may wonder how you ended up with so many new friends with children. We enjoy being around like-minded people, and there is nothing wrong with that.

The flip side is that similarity bias can cause us to resist connections with people who are not similar to us and take interest only in those who are. Hiring managers especially should be careful of this bias because it will lead them to hire in their own image. If an organization doesn't check this behavior, it can easily end up being a company of people who all think and behave the same. Have you ever heard the statement "He reminds me so much of myself"? This is an indication of similarity bias.

Halo and Horns Effects

The *halo effect* is when a characteristic we like about a person influences our opinions on everything else about that person. The *horns effect* is when we perceive one negative thing about a person and the "horns" of that one thing influences our opinion about that person. These biases are two sides of the same coin. When we like someone, they can do no wrong. When we don't like someone, they can do no right. Halo and horns effects show up often with celebrities. If you love LeBron James and think he's the greatest of all time, especially considering how well he connects with others and shows love to his family, it might be hard for you to admit when he's having a tough game day. On the other side, though, say you think LeBron James is incredibly arrogant, self-serving—and who refers to themselves as "King," anyway?—well, you can spot all the missteps LeBron makes with ease. Pick your favorite celeb or the celeb you love to hate and try this; sound familiar?

Halo and horns effects play out in real life. We find reasons to not give promotions and opportunities to people with those horns and will create opportunities for people who have halos. These effects can be a real source of favoritism or discrimination in workplaces or shared spaces.

Bias happens to everyone. You can't escape it. I always tell my clients we are all biasing all over everywhere, all the time. There is no removing all bias because it is wired into how our brains work. So, are you biased? Yes! We all are. The word "bias" has a negative connotation, but, in reality, it does plenty of good in our lives. However, because acting on a bias can also be inappropriate, discriminatory, or offensive, we need to check biased behaviors and be open when someone tells us we are being biased. Rather than taking offense, a more appropriate response is to ask "Can you help me see what I am missing?" so you can become aware of potential biased behavior that could be doing harm.

Before we transition to the next chapter, I want you to do a quick exercise. Pull out a sheet of paper and make a list of ten people you trust who are not immediate family. (Immediate family is anyone you have ever lived in a home with.) Not life-or-death trust, but reasonable trust. You'd invite them to your home for a meal or you know they'd stop if they saw you on the side of the road. I know we have been sheltering in place for a while so it might be a little hard to think about. Maybe pull out your phone. But make sure you have ten people.

Got your list?

Great. Set it aside or tuck it in this book. We will to come back to it later.

Questions to Consider

1. Did you learn anything new about inclusion? If so, what did you learn?
2. Can you think of your own examples of conformity bias in your own life? Take a moment and describe the scenario to yourself or someone you know. Can you do the same for similarity bias? Halo and horns effect?
3. Have you encountered unconscious bias before? What was the situation?

9 Microaggressions

Microaggressions are small or subtle behaviors that occur in casual encounters that judge, accuse, demean, marginalize, or show prejudice toward someone. Microaggressions are experienced as minor verbal or nonverbal actions that can discount a person, single someone out, or belittle someone based on a part of their identity, such as age, race, or gender. Microaggressions can be deliberate or unintentional.

The term "microaggressions" falls under a broader category of behavior called micromessaging. Micromessaging includes several other terms, such as microinequities, microinsults, microaffirmations, and microinvalidations. What all of these terms all have in common is that they are indicated by small behaviors, as the prefix "micro-" suggests. Note that, many times, people call any micromessage a microaggression, and, honestly, that is okay. The specificity of the term isn't as important as understanding how micromessages present in our encounters with others and what the behaviors associated with them suggest.

Microaggressions are small behaviors, but they are considered aggressive because of their frequency. The impact of microaggressions is cumulative. Imagine if every single day your neighbor greets you by the wrong name as you head to your mailbox. Every day you correct them and pronounce your name. Every day they apologize, and then a few days later, they say your name wrong again. Your neighbor doesn't see the big deal; they just can't remember how to pronounce your name, that's all. For you, though, it's a nuisance, and it may make you not want to speak to the neighbor anymore. You may even go out of your way to avoid them. The impact on you builds up over time. When someone encounters the same small slight over and over, it feels more impactful each time it happens. It could be as simple as people mispronouncing your name. People might even minimize you pushing back by saying something like "Your name is so hard to pronounce" and then continuing to call you by the wrong name. The act itself is small, but the frequency of the experience makes it feel aggressive to the receiver. Another issue with microaggressions is that the receiver can get so fed up over time that they ultimately take their frustration out on someone who innocently commits the microaggression for the first time.

How do microaggressions show up? They present themselves in a number of ways, including tone, body language, and word choice to name a few. Let's look at a few examples to make sure it is clear how microaggressions can show up.

Read the following sentences aloud and put emphasis on the italicized word:

I didn't *say* Amber isn't performing well.

I didn't say *Amber* isn't performing well.

Did you notice that while the sentences contain the same words, they send different messages depending on which word was emphasized? The first sentence suggests that Amber isn't performing well, but the speaker didn't necessarily say that aloud. Perhaps the speaker suggested it or alluded to it in some other way. The second sentence is suggesting someone isn't performing well, but it is not Amber. Tone is a common means of sending micromessages and being microaggressive, then gaslighting (manipulation that causes someone to question their own sanity) the receiver of the message. The receiving party may respond to the micromessage, and the person who said the message may pretend to not be aware of the micromessage. Using the second example above, someone may respond by saying "Well, who isn't performing well?" to which the person who initiated the micromessage may say, "What makes you think someone isn't performing well? I didn't say someone wasn't performing well." Technically, they would be correct; they did not say someone wasn't performing well. They micromessaged it with their tone by strategically placing emphasis in a certain place.

Body language also can display microaggressions. Imagine you are the only woman on your team. Every time you walk into your leader's office to speak with them, they never look up from their computer. Sure, the leader answers your questions or addresses what you need support with, but they never seem attentive. However, when one of the men on your team goes in to speak with the leader, the leader gives them their full attention, including eye contact and inviting body language. You even notice they exchange personal stories and playful banter. This is a microaggression; with the leader's body language, they are sending the message, "I am not open to discussion with the woman on my team." The leader may not even be aware of it, but microaggressions can happen without someone intending to offend.

Microaggressions can be physical interactions as well. I have seen people reach out and touch someone's hair out of curiosity. I have seen people put their arm up against another person's arm in comparison of skin tones or ask someone "Do you have to tan?" Another example of a microaggression is clutching your belongings when a Black person joins you on an elevator. Physical interactions that call out aspects of someone's identity or make some characteristic of theirs seem abnormal might fall into the category of a microaggression.

Microaggressions can also show up in sentence structure, messaging, and word choice. Telling someone "Mateo works in construction. He is a Latino engineer" is a microaggression. The sentences are just as effective stated as "Mateo is an engineer working in construction." The intentional call out of "Latino" suggests that Latino people are not engineers, which leads someone to point it out. It is a microaggression. It suggests "Here is something different you haven't seen before," which can feel uncomfortable for people who worked hard to be where they are in their lives.

Many microaggressions are statements people make. Table 9.1 is a chart of a few common microaggressive statements, including a few of those covered earlier. I have also included why the statement might be perceived as offensive and microaggressive.

It is important to remember that just because you do not find something to be a microaggression or otherwise offensive, it doesn't mean that someone else will not find it offensive. Offense is largely subjective and based on personal experience. As we discussed in Chapter 7, we alone know our identity. Others may experience it, but we define it for ourselves. Others define their identity for themselves as well. If someone finds something you said or did to be a microaggression, they alone know their experience. So, it may feel very small to you, because you might not encounter microaggressions. However, your reality is not everyone's reality. We should make room for the possibility

Table 9.1: A Few Common Microaggressive Statements

Microaggression	Message
■ "Where is your family from?" ■ "What are you mixed with?" ■ "You look so exotic."	**Alien in own land** You are not from America or you look like your parents are from another place.
■ "You are so articulate!" ■ Asking a tall Black man if he plays basketball ■ Asking an Asian person if they are good at math	**Questioning intelligence** People of color are not as intelligent as Whites.
■ "You people . . ." ■ Assuming a Black or Brown person is a service worker or wait staff	**Lower-class citizen** You are a lesser person than I am.
■ Asking a woman when she is going to get married or have a baby	**Diminishment of worth** Your womanhood is not enough.
■ "I couldn't even tell you were gay!" ■ "You don't look Native American." ■ "You don't look like a doctor."	**Reducing identity to what is perceived** Your identity isn't visible. Your identity isn't valid because I cannot identify it.

that someone else is having a different experience. In chapter 16, we dig into what to do if you overhear a microaggression, treat someone else microaggressively, or are the recipient of a microaggression.

Questions to Consider

1. What are some microaggressions you have encountered? How did you handle the encounter?
2. Did you have any "aha" moments about microaggressions while reading this chapter? If so, what were they?
3. Microaggressions are small behaviors, so why do they have such a big impact?

10 Equality and Equity

Fair treatment is one of the major experiences that marginalized and underrepresented groups are seeking, but what is fair isn't always clear. You may hear folks make statements like "We should treat all people equally, regardless of the color of their skin." Simultaneously, you might hear the word "equity" in messages that companies make about racial justice or pay. The words "equality" and "equity" at times work together, but they mean different things. As an ally, it is helpful to know in what circumstances you want to push for equity and when equality is the objective. Let's explore these two terms with a few simple examples.

Equality is the state of being equal. It means that everyone is treated the same in terms of rights, status, and opportunities. Equality does not consider if people have different needs; it ensures that everyone gets the same thing. An example of equality is making sure everyone on the team who works seven hours or more gets a full one-hour lunch break. No one has to do anything special or apply; they will be treated equally and receive a one-hour lunch break. Often, when we are considering equality, we are speaking about several people experiencing something, not individuals.

Equity is about fairness in the way people are treated. It considers the unique needs of each person when determining how to treat or support someone. Equity considers that everyone does not have the same starting place and may need something different depending on their unique circumstances. Imagine you plan on serving lunch during the lunch break described earlier. Equity considers "How much food do I need? Does anyone have dietary restrictions? Is the space we are hosting lunch in accessible to everyone, even those who may be disabled?" Equity is often more focused on the individual or a specific group's experience.

The popular illustration in Figure 10.1 demonstrates equity and equality in a very simple way. For the equality side, everyone gets a crate to stand on at the game, but for one of the people, the crate is not enough because they are still too short to see over the fence. On the equity side, the people get the number of crates they need in order to see the game, resulting in the shortest character having two crates and the tall character having none.

Equality and equity have their respective meanings but also operate in some of the same spaces. For example, the legal system seems like an ideal place for equal treatment; if you are found guilty of "x" crime, the penalty is "y" for everyone. Ideally the legal system should treat people equally. In reality, the justice system treats poor people inequitably based on their financial status. Money, race, and even political affiliation can play a part in how people in the United States experience the justice system. Inequities in the justice system result in unequal treatment.

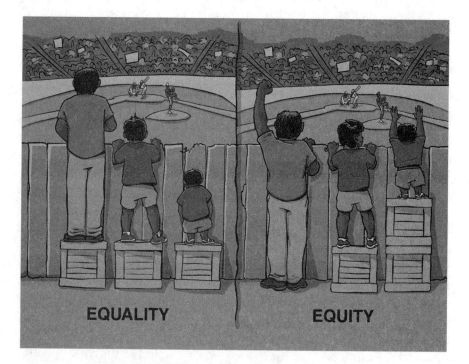

Figure 10.1: Comparison of equality and equity

Source: Courtesy of the Interaction Institute for Social Change | Artist: Angus Maguire

Another example is pay inequity, which has been a pretty popular and mainstream conversation the last few years, with even political candidates touting their plans to address the gender pay gap. Pay inequity specifically speaks about the pay gaps that exist across race and gender, leading White men to be the highest paid and all other identities falling behind them. Pay equity calls for all identities doing a job with the same qualifications to be paid *equally* regardless of their identity. Currently, anyone not White and male experiences an *inequity* because their pay is correlated with other aspects of identity that have nothing to do with their ability to do a job.

Underrepresented identities and groups experience unequal and inequitable treatment in a number of ways. As an ally and an advocate, becoming familiar with the ways inequity and inequality present for the people you are supporting can help you do a better job of changing experiences and challenging oppression against underrepresented people.

Questions to Consider

1. In your own words, explain "equality" and "equity."
2. What are some circumstances you can think of where equity applies? What are some circumstances where equality applies?

Privilege

11

L et's start with this. We all have privilege of some kind. The word "privilege" sometimes has a negative connotation, as people told they have privilege usually assume that the speaker thinks they have not met with any challenges in life. Here's the thing about privilege: You can have a lot of it, and, first, not realize it and, second, still have faced a lot of challenges in your life. Privileges are rights, advantages, or protections granted to or accessible by a particular person or group of people. If you are right-handed, that is a privilege. Ask any lefty; they will tell you all about the ways a right-handed world presents challenges. If you have running water, that is a privilege. If you are able-bodied, you have privilege. Literally every single person has some sort of privileges. There is no reason to deny having privilege, because you have it. We all do. Privilege is helpful to us. Depending on the kind of privilege, it can give you a leg up, it can make life easier, it can open doors, or it can even give you a greater sense of safety.

Let's do a quick exercise. Place a check mark next to each statement that applies to you.

PRIVILEGE CHECKLIST

- ■ I am right-handed.
- ■ I grew up in a two-parent household.
- ■ I attended a private school growing up.
- ■ I have never worried about my electricity, water, or gas being shut off.
- ■ I never had to help my parents with the bills when I was growing up.

- I didn't have to pay for college (not due to athletic ability).
- I never had to worry about when I would have my next meal.
- My family had health insurance growing up.
- The traditional US work holidays coincide with the holidays that I celebrate (Independence Day, Christmas, etc.).
- I studied the culture of my ancestors while in elementary school.
- My family owned the house where I grew up.
- My parents or guardians attended college.
- I took family vacations or went to camp as a child.
- I was encouraged to attend college by my parents.
- I have never had to consider my complexion when shopping for bandages or makeup.
- I have never had to consider my gender when going out alone at night.
- I have never had to consider my sexuality when thinking about getting married or having children.
- I never fear for my life when I am stopped by the police for a traffic stop.
- I have often had leaders who looked like me. (If you are in school, replace "leaders" with "teachers.")
- I don't have to think about what restroom to use when I am in public.
- I have never been followed in a place of business.

How many checked boxes did you have? I have six. How do you feel about the number of boxes you checked? When people have a lot of checkmarks, sometimes they feel guilty. Maybe they weren't aware of their privileges, or they feel bad that they have more than others. Privilege is not a reason to feel guilty. Often our most helpful privileges have very little to do with decisions we have made for ourselves. Being able to identify your own privileges, though, can help you to be an ally and an advocate. Allyship is when someone with *privilege* and power seeks to learn about the experiences of a marginalized group of people, develops empathy for them, and identifies ways to extend their privilege to the marginalized group. An advocate is someone with *privilege* and power who seeks to protect, publicly support, and dismantle systems against a marginalized group of people. As the definitions suggest, allyship and advocacy require some awareness of your privilege. There is no need to feel guilty about your privileges; instead, lean into the work of being an ally and an advocate for marginalized people who don't experience the privileges you do.

Conversely, some people check very few boxes in this exercise, and instead of guilt, they feel shame or embarrassment. Looking at the list can feel like a running tally of privileges that could have made a big impact on how they experience their own lives. Lack of privilege is not a reason to feel shame or embarrassment either. Again, many of the decisions that led to you not having privilege are not decisions you made; instead, they are aspects of your identity or the products of your upbringing. It is possible that you are also a part of a marginalized group. That's okay too. You still have the ability to be an ally and an advocate. You still have the ability to decide to be an ally and learn about the experiences of marginalized groups who experience life in a different way from you, and extended your privilege to them. You still can protect, advocate for, and dismantle systems against people.

There are many more things that I could add to the list of statements above. Had I switched a few of the statements out for others, you might have had many more or many fewer check marks. All that demonstrates is that privilege is a matter of perspective. Depending on what perspective we take, we will see different privileges we do or do not have. Since many of us don't appreciate what having privilege connotes, we sometimes respond to uncovering our privilege by recalling the many obstacles we have faced. The two are not mutually exclusive: We can both have privilege and be challenged.

A few types of privilege are talked about frequently because of how significantly they can improve a person's quality of life. Financial privilege is one type. People who have great wealth have access to many things that people without wealth do not. Some examples include day-to-day experiences, such as access to elite schools and private air travel, as well as social and institutional access, including the ability to influence municipal decisions.

White privilege is another type of privilege that has an impact on a person's quality of life. White privilege is favoritism, advantages, and protections granted to White people. Benefits of White privilege include preferential treatment, being seen as the norm, and being exempt from experiencing group oppression. Sometimes White people struggle to see their own privilege, or they are uncomfortable with the idea that the way they experience life would be considered privileged. Remember, though, privilege is a matter of perspective. When we look at how White people experience the world compared to how others do, it is easy to see the preferential treatment and advantages. Next are a few relevant life examples:

- According to a 2017 report by the United States Sentencing Commission, White men who commit the same crimes as Black men receive federal prison sentences that are, on average, nearly 20% shorter.[1]
- In the second quarter of 2020, even with historic unemployment rates across the United States, the median weekly earnings of Blacks ($806) and Hispanics ($786) working at full-time jobs were lower than those of Whites ($1,018) and Asians ($1,336) according to the Bureau of Labor Statistics.[2]
- The National Institute of Standards and Technology found in 2019 that facial recognition software misidentifies people of color up to 100 times as often as White men.[3]
- White people have the privilege of learning about racism and choosing whether to believe it rather than having to experience it in their lives.
- Eighty percent of teachers and 84% of full-time college professors in the United States are White.[4] If you are White, you are more likely to be taught by someone who looks like you.

---

[1]United States Sentencing Commission, "Demographic Differences in Sentencing: An Update to the 2012 *Booker* Report," November 2017, https://www.ussc.gov/sites/default/files/pdf/research-and-publications/research-publications/2017/20171114_Demographics.pdf

[2]Bureau of Labor Statistics, US Department of Labor, "Usual Weekly Earnings of Wage and Salary Workers Second Quarter 2020," Press release, USDL-20-1380, https://www.bls.gov/news.release/pdf/wkyeng.pdf

[3]Drew Harwell, "Federal Study Confirms Racial Bias of Many Facial-Recognition Systems, Casts Doubt on Their Expanding Use," *Washington Post*, December 19, 2019, https://www.washingtonpost.com/technology/2019/12/19/federal-study-confirms-racial-bias-many-facial-recognition-systems-casts-doubt-their-expanding-use/

[4]National Center for Education Statistics, "Spotlight A: Characteristics of Public School Teachers by Race/Ethnicity," February 2019, https://nces.ed.gov/programs/raceindicators/spotlight_a.asp; and National Center for Education Statistics, "Fast Facts: Race/Ethnicity of College Faculty," https://nces.ed.gov/fastfacts/display.asp?id=61

- Congress is 78 percent White. If you are White, people in positions of power making laws and decisions about your life and your community identify similarly to you.

Did these statistics surprise you? If not, consider reading them again, but this time change "White" to "Black."

White privilege does not mean that everything a White person has achieved or accomplished was not earned or deserved. It does mean that there is a system of built-in advantage for White people that is separate from their hard work and effort.

Identifying our own privilege is not easy. Privilege makes us so comfortable and becomes our norm so we don't even consider how we might experience the world. When it is called to our attention, we may feel accused because we equate privilege with having an easy life or not being hard working, neither of which are true. Having White privilege and recognizing it is the behavior of allies and advocates who are eager to use their privilege to create a more equitable system.

Questions to Consider

1. What are some privileges you identified in the exercise at the start of the chapter? Were there certain statements that were more impactful than others?
2. If you could add some additional statements to the privilege walk, what would you add?
3. Why is privilege not a reason to feel ashamed or guilty?

12 System, Systemic, Systematic

I use the word "system" a lot in this book, so let's explore what the word is referring to in context of inclusion and equity work. "System" refers to the policies and practices entrenched in established institutions and society that result in the exclusion of or the promotion of designated groups. You can think of it as the prescription or directions we follow to have an orderly or normal life. We don't even think about it, we just follow the system.

There are many systems at play that give us the policies and procedures that we follow. In Chapter 13 we will talk about systems of oppression, but systems do more than oppress; they give us frameworks to follow. We have educational systems to validate our learning and skills; legal systems to determine right and wrong as well as penalize violators of right and wrong; medical systems to diagnose, treat, and study illness. All of these, and many more, systems are normal parts of everyday life. Many times we don't even think about them. We participate and benefit from systems, often without realizing that the way they work for us may not be the way they work for others.

As an example, a student whose family has a lot of money has access to a different educational system experience from one whose family does not. Since the wealthy student's experience sent them to expensive schools, they may develop the belief that someone who went to a less expensive university is less qualified, less educated, or less capable than they are and treat them differently. Conversely, students who had to take out loans to go to school and worked full time may have a different view of educational systems. They may look at other skills and life experiences when assessing other people, not just education, because their experiences may lead them to believe that since everyone doesn't have equal access to the educational system, it is an unfair to make educational experience a sole measure of qualification, intellect, or capability. Systems work on all of us, and we participate at varying levels.

There are a couple of terms that you might have been hearing lately in regard to "the system" that are important to understand when thinking about inclusion and diversity work. The terms are "systematic" and "systemic."

"Systematic" means thorough, methodical, and intentional actions or steps as a part of a system. The term speaks of something that consists of a system or a specific series of steps that are followed to get to a result. Let's explore a couple of examples.

In 2018, a medical school in Japan admitted to systematically lowering the scores of women who took the school's entrance exam while giving bonus points to men to boost their scores. The school systematically lowered the scores of women—just because they were women—to keep them from getting into medical school. This practice had been going on for over a decade. The process of lowering a score based on an identity attribute is a systematic process. It is one step in a system that can be corrected by stopping (or starting) a behavior or action.

Another example is a recruiter dismissing any resumes with ethnic- or Black-sounding names. In this case, the recruiter is taking a specific step to remove certain people from the candidate pool. The action of dismissing a resume based on a name is systematic. It is one step in the hiring system that can be corrected by stopping (or starting) a behavior or action.

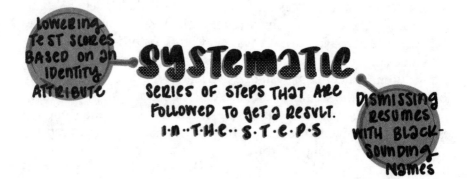

The term "systemic" is a bit more complex. "Systemic" means something is a widespread policy or practice that is entrenched in the institution, practice, or system. It means there isn't a specific step that can be identified and changed or removed; whatever is happening is entangled in the process. Therefore, the outcomes are common or normal to that system. Let's explore a couple of examples of systemic policies.

In the 1930s, the Home Owners Loan Corporation, a government-sponsored company, determined a neighborhood's risk for loan default and outlined them on a map, a process known as redlining. The redlined neighborhoods were largely Black neighborhoods, making Black people ineligible for housing loans, while White middle-class Americans were able to receive housing loans. White families began moving into suburbs, where they could find affordable and high-quality housing, while property in or near Black neighborhoods was considered high risk, making securing loans for property in these areas impossible. The appraisal process of the Federal Housing Association (FHA) also incentivized White families who secured housing in the suburbs to keep Blacks out of those suburban neighborhoods. The FHA Underwriting Manual gave instructions to keep loan rates in suburban communities low that included avoiding "infiltration by inharmonious racial or nationality groups." These federally funded lending practices essentially forced Black neighborhoods to deteriorate because no one could secure money to invest in their survival. Black people could not leave the deteriorating area because they could not access loans in areas marked as free from "infiltration by inharmonious racial or nationality groups."

This is only a part of a very complicated story about property laws and home loans in the United States, but let's examine this part for a moment. The housing loan story is systemic because the issue is embedded in the process. There is not one easily identifiable single step that caused the segregation of neighborhoods in the United States; the entire system was rife with racist practices. There is no one clear step to remove to stop the racist practices. The racism is systemic and so entrenched in the process that if you were a White person, you had no reason to even notice. You wanted a home, you could get one in a nice community. Why would you even consider living in or near an area that is deteriorating? So people are participating in a system that is creating the very deterioration they do not want to live near. Complex, right? Can you see how easy it is to participate in systemic oppression and believe you are just doing what is good and right for you or your family?

Here is another way systemic racism might show up. A graduate of Harvard and another from MIT come together and form a company. The company starts to grow and is profitable, so the founders need to do some hiring. They decide, "Let's establish hiring relationships with our schools." They feel good about the quality of the education they received, so they believe it's a good idea to hire from those schools. They see it as a way to hire quality candidates and give back to their schools. Over the next five years, the majority of their staff of 200 are hires from either Harvard or MIT. Since the company has hiring relationships with the schools, students from Harvard and MIT are considered earlier and are a higher priority than outside applicants because the founders want to meet the terms of their hiring agreements with the schools. Can you see how, in an effort to do a good thing, the founders have created a system that excludes certain candidates and looks for certain criteria that aren't necessarily an indicator of skill to build their workforce?

Is it wrong to establish a hiring relationship with a school? No. Several years down the line, though, even if the company ends the hiring relationship, because there are so many hires from MIT and Harvard, the same standards will continue to apply. The mindset of the hiring system will be challenging to change. It is not one specific thing. It would be easy for someone to say "I didn't hire her because she is from MIT, I hired her because she is good," but the system has defined the attributes that come with MIT grads as the standard for good hires.

Fixing systemic discrimination requires people to commit to seeing the problem and being willing to break the system altogether and build something better. That process might be disruptive, expensive, and even uncomfortable. The difficulties make it really easy to decide not to address systemic discrimination. After all, the system works for some people—especially if it works for you.

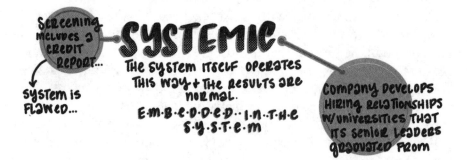

Screening includes a credit report...

system is FLAWED...

SYSTEMIC

The system itself operates this way + the results are normal.

E·m·b·e·d·d·e·d··i·n··t·h·e s·y·s·t·e·m

company develops hiring relationships w/ universities that its senior leaders graduated from

These examples show how equity work isn't a personal attack on anyone. However, you are complicit in perpetuating many systems because every system requires (and operates on) your participation, even if you do not like it. We are all a part of the system and the subsystems that comprise it. You are participating in racism, colorism, sexism, and much more. We all are. Allies are able to recognize and admit that these systems exist and take steps in their own lives to disrupt the systems or address the injustices caused because of them.

Next, let's dig into some of the most common systems of oppression and discuss how and why you are part of them, even when you don't mean to be.

-Isms and -Ist

In this chapter we discuss some of the subsystems that we are all participating in that continue to keep the system, along with systemic and systematic oppression, in operation today.

-Isms

You have probably heard of the most common -isms:

- Racism
- Classism
- Colorism
- Heterosexism (also known as homophobia)
- Ableism
- Ageism
- Anti-Semitism

There are many more. In the context of inclusion and diversity, -isms such as these are indicators that there is a system of privilege and power at play. We defined "privilege" as rights, advantages, or protections granted to or accessible by a particular person or group of people. Power in this circumstance is the ability to exert authority over, influence, or direct another individual's or group's experience. A teacher has power and privilege in a classroom of students, for example. If students desire high marks, they behave in ways that will produce those results according to the standard set by the teacher. Teachers have rights and protections afforded to them because they are teachers, especially if they are a part of a teacher's union. Power and privilege do not always have negative associations. You have power and privilege over many aspects of your own life, and those powers and privileges are not bad or negative. However, there are some systems of privilege and power that make life harder for people. These systems are the -isms.

-Isms play on power systems, and that is what keeps them in place. In every -ism there is a power system at play. The group with the power is the group that can oppress, discriminate against, or obstruct without the likelihood of suffering repercussions for their behavior. Using our teacher example, imagine a teacher giving students low marks unfairly. It would take a lot for the students to prove what is happening and have the teacher removed. Even if they did have the teacher removed, the teacher likely would be able to be hired at another school in another area without issue.

It is important to note how -isms work so you can understand why things like "reverse racism" or "reverse classism" do not exist. The oppressed group may very well be prejudiced or discriminate against someone with power, but their ability to oppress them is limited. The students in the example would be extremely limited in oppressing the teacher. Black people do not have the social or institutional power to oppress White people. Women do not have the social or institutional power to oppress men. The power dynamic is key in systems of oppression or -isms.

Let's use colorism as an example to show how -isms embed themselves into our lives in ways that can make us all complicit in the system.

Colorism is a system of prejudice or discrimination against individuals with a dark skin tone and favoritism or access for individuals with a light skin tone. Colorism typically happens among people in the same ethnic or racial group. The origins of colorism date back hundreds of years. During slavery in the United States, light-skinned Black people did work in the master's house while brown- and dark-skinned Black people were left to do backbreaking work in the heat of the plantation fields. The ranking of complexion, where closer to White is viewed as "good," has set up a systemic hierarchy that is alive and well today interculturally around the globe. Brown- and dark-skinned people have bleached their skin and even lightened their eyes to appear closer to a socially defined ideal complexion that will give them more favor.

In the system of colorism, brown- and dark-skinned people are mistreated and oppressed. Dark-skinned people are seen as less intelligent, less beautiful, and even less capable of achieving. Light-skinned people have favor and preferential treatment in the colorism system.

Light-skinned people are seen as "good Black people," viewed as being beautiful or exotic and given opportunities not available to people with dark skin. I want to make sure it is clear that all complexions participate in the system, sometimes unknowingly. However, only brown- and dark-skinned people are *oppressed* by colorism; light-skinned people have *favoritism*, which amounts to power and privilege, because of it.

In the system of colorism, I am a light-skinned woman, so I have privilege and power. Here is what that looks like for me:

- Very often because of my complexion, people assume that I am not Black, so I am met with courtesy or even curiosity instead of resistance. This is a global phenomenon. In every country I visit, without fail someone attempts to speak to me in the local language.
- I am very often seen as and referred to as beautiful by Black men, in contrast to browner women. I am often referred to as "stereotypically beautiful" and "exotic."
- I can always find a "nude" bandage, tights, or makeup in my local pharmacy that will look fine against my skin.
- I have been told I am "not like other Black people" because I come across "approachable" and my appearance isn't "hard."
- My last name is a name chosen two generations ago to allow my family to pass. My last name actually should be McCoy. Most of my family is light-skinned, and many have at varying points passed for White.
- I can readily find doctors, teachers, and even actors and actresses in whom I can see my own identity.

All of these things may be seemingly small, but they add up to access to privileges and opportunity that I can receive by doing nothing more than showing up. Even if I don't want to be, I am a beneficiary of colorism. At times, I am not trusted or am met with skepticism by brown- and dark-skinned Black people because they wonder if I am actually Black or just passing for Black. I have been called "half White" more times than I can count, and I am often reminded of the kinds of favoritism and access I receive because I am light-skinned. These things are disappointing and, sure, at times they are hurtful. However, they are very minor in comparison to the impacts of colorism on brown-skinned and dark-skinned Black people.

- People do not assume that I do not belong somewhere or assume the worst about me as the only Black person in the room. I am never mistaken for a cleaning staff or service person.
- People do not fetishize my complexion, try to touch my skin, or take offense at my skin tone.
- Brown- and dark-skinned women have been told by men they are "pretty for a dark-skinned girl."
- Brown- and dark-skinned people have to special order or visit multiple stores to find nude shades of clothing, makeup, or shoes to match their skin tone.
- Brown- and dark-skinned people have been called derogatory terms like "darkie," "monkey," or "blue-black" to describe them or their complexion.
- Parents have "the talk" about how to safely engage with police with brown- and dark-skinned children. They do not have the same discussion with their light-skinned children.
- Finding doctors, teachers, actors, and actresses who are dark-skinned is a challenge, which can suggest to a brown- or dark-skinned person that they aren't able to do or participate in certain careers.

Experiences like these tell brown- or dark-skinned people that they are ugly, unloved, undesirable, and unwanted. The experiences message in subtle or direct ways that a brown- or dark-skinned person's identity is worthless because they are not light enough. While living in my own light skin, I may encounter hurtful or disappointing experiences. However, to move to the place of allyship and advocacy, it is important to realize that hurtful and disappointing experiences, while valid, do not compare to feeling undervalued or worthless. As a beneficiary of the colorism system who wants to disrupt and challenge the status quo as an ally to brown- and dark-skinned people, I have to understand my feelings are my feelings, but I have favor even if I didn't ask for it. My priority as an ally and an advocate is centering the feelings and perspectives of those who are victimized and oppressed by colorism.

Imagine a world where you cannot make a quick run to the pharmacy to pick up what you need. Imagine arriving at a resort for vacation and being mistaken for housekeeping staff. Imagine looking for a doctor for a serious condition and not finding anyone who looks like you.

We all participate in a number of systems, whether we want to or not. We participate in behaviors and practices that are embedded into our day-to-day lives that uphold the system of colorism, sexism, and even racism. We may receive privilege in some systems and be oppressed by others. We may personally believe colorism, sexism, or racism are wrong. However, the systems are so pervasive that everyone is complicit—even underrepresented or oppressed people in the system—in upholding the standards that keep the systems in place. The degree to which we are all participating is what makes these systems challenging to dismantle and makes doing so a long-term undertaking. We cannot begin to dismantle oppressive systems until people are willing to be allies and advocates who understand that our own feelings and comfort are not always the priority.

For many people, the idea that our own comfort shouldn't take center stage is a challenging one. If you find it difficult to consider that your comfort isn't always supposed to be a priority, consider a couple things we discussed in Part I of this book:

- Growth comes from discomfort. If you are unwilling to be uncomfortable, it means you are unwilling to grow and you will not be able to be an ally or an advocate for others.
- If your priority is always your own comfort, when does the discomfort of someone else matter? How will you be able to develop the empathy and connectivity to connect to others who are experiencing oppression?

Most people find power systems and -isms difficult topics because they touch on some very personal identity aspects—things many of us feel are fundamental to who we are or that we cannot change. When you encounter mistreatment and discrimination directed toward others, sometimes it is helpful to identify for yourself what power system is at play so you can call behavior by its name. Identifying the power system also can help you to identify who has privilege. If that is you, it may give you clues on how you can use your privilege to be an ally or advocate. Next are some definitions for a few other common -isms:

- Ableism is a system of prejudice or discrimination against people who are disabled (sometimes called differently abled) based on the belief that people with typical abilities are superior.

- Ageism is a system of prejudice or discrimination against people's age based on the idea that being a certain age means you are inferior or superior. Ageism typically is directed toward older adults, but in recent years the term has been applied to younger people, even though young people are not recognized as a marginalized group.
- Anti-Semitism is discrimination or prejudice against Jews.
- Classism is a system of prejudice or discrimination against people of a certain social class in favor of people of another social class. A common example of classism is that celebrities are treated differently in restaurants from people who are not well recognized.
- Featurism is a system of prejudice or discrimination against people who have Afrocentric features, like wide noses, full lips, curvaceous bodies, and hair with small, tight curls. Featurism favors people with Eurocentric features, such as small, straight noses, small lips, and straight hair or loose curls.
- Heterosexism (also known as homophobia) is a system of prejudice or discrimination against homosexual people based on the idea that heterosexuality is normal.
- Racism is a system of prejudice or discrimination against people of a certain race rooted in social and institutional power combined with racial privilege. Racism operates on the belief that the race with social and institutional power is superior. When racism is specifically directed toward Black people, it is sometimes referred to as anti-Black racism.
- Sexism is a system of prejudice or discrimination by the dominant gender (usually men) against another gender (usually women).
- Tokenism is the act of doing something or giving visibility to someone to prevent criticism or to give the appearance of inclusion or equity. An example is hiring a woman senior vice president and ensuring she is very visible to avoid criticism that the leadership team is all male. People who are in the role of the token may or may not know they are being tokenized. With tokenism, the power is held by the person who put the token in place because they are the decision maker and are using someone to maintain power and social standing. The token is the oppressed person, whether they know it or not, because their power rests in their placement.

-Ist

Words that end in -ist are probably familiar to you as well. They are terms many people find offensive and try to avoid. Some common -ist words are:

- Racist
- Classist
- Colorist
- Sexist
- Ageist
- Ableist
- Heterosexist (homophobic)

Terms that end in -ist are used to identify the culprit or the action that produces the oppressive or discriminatory behavior of an -ism—for example, "The questionnaire is ageist" or "My brother is homophobic." The -ist words identify who or what committed the -ism. -Ist words can apply only to the person with the power in that system. Going back to our colorism example, as a light-skinned Black woman, I can be colorist toward brown-skinned Black people. A colorist remark might sound like this: "He is very dark-skinned but still handsome." The statement implies that dark-skinned people are not typically handsome people.

In each system, the oppressed person is the individual with no power in that system—so a gay man who does not like gay men is not homophobic, because he has no power over gay people. Instead, he is prejudiced against gay people. A Black person who does not like Black people is not racist, because even if they do not like Black people, they are impacted by the same oppression as other Black people. A Black person who discriminates against Black people is instead prejudiced against Black people.

There are many layers to our identities, so, as a result, we may be oppressed by one or more systems and simultaneously receive favor in others. For example, a dark-skinned Latino man who is gay and able-bodied might play several roles in systems of oppression. As an able-bodied man, he has privileges over someone who is disabled and over women. As a dark-skinned person who is gay, he is subject to be oppressed by White people, light-skinned Latinx people, and heterosexual people.

When you have the power in a system—White, light-skinned, heterosexual, traditionally physically abled, young, practice a traditional religion, et cetera—it does not mean you do not encounter challenges or have not had bad things happen to you in your life. It is even possible that you have encountered some difficulties related to your privilege. You get to have whatever emotions you have about these things, and all of that is normal.

However, it is really important that you recognize that even if you cannot see the system immediately or are still learning to identify it, systems of oppression have a great impact on how those impacted or oppressed by the system experience life, safety, and access to opportunity. Remember, we may not always see the many ways we have social, institutional, and economic power. Our power and privilege can be hard for us to notice because they make us comfortable.

Historically, -ism and -ist words are trigger words for people and cause them to get defensive. It may feel that the right behavior is to avoid these words altogether, but we know speaking up and using our candor is allyship and advocate behavior. Do the brave thing: Call behaviors that uphold systems of oppression what they are—racism, sexism, anti-Semitism, and so on. Saying the right word and understanding its meaning helps others to learn to identify these behaviors as well. We can all do our part to dismantle systems of oppression, but making sure we are brave enough to talk about it, using the right words, is an essential first step.

Engaging with Others

It is one thing to be reading this book learning about challenging topics, but it's an entirely different thing to be engaging with others out in the world. I know it's a little scary, but the fear and nervousness is part of being an ally and an advocate. What happens if someone calls you racist? Or homophobic? How should you respond? Here are some tips to engage:

- All of these words are trigger words; they are not slurs. They are words that mean things we do not like or want to be accused of. Don't let your emotions run away with you. Remember, the words are triggering and you do not have to be triggered. Someone is reacting to a thing you did, not a thing you are.

- Do not get defensive. Don't say "I am not racist!" or "Don't address me that way." Doing that isn't helpful. Push past the defensive energy; we need to get to a solution. Count to ten in your mind to remain calm if you need to, but don't get defensive. We will never dismantle any systems from a position of defense.
- Listen for and identify the root concern. Use eye contact and body language to show you are listening.
- Once you identify the root issue, acknowledge it. The phrases "I understand" and "I see your perspective" are helpful here. Remember to consider "If this were true, how would I respond?" or "If this were my favorite person in the world, how would I respond?"
- If an apology is due, apologize. "I apologize for _____. Moving forward I will _____."
- Avoid explanations or examples. So, no "What I meant was . . ." or "But my best friend is Black." None of that matters in the heat of the moment.
- Keep what you found valuable about the discussion and discard the rest. Every tough conversation is an opportunity for you to both practice and learn.

Will these steps work every time? Unfortunately, no. However, they will help you to be prepared for and manage a challenging discussion, even if it doesn't follow these exact steps. There will be times when you will need to make the decision to responsibly exit a discussion where you are not being heard. There will be times where the person accusing you is looking for an argument. Whatever the scenario, making sure that you aren't set off by a trigger word is a great step toward having a healthy discussion with someone who is looking to engage with integrity.

White Supremacy

White supremacy is a very controversial topic that is also deeply entrenched in American and even global history. For the purposes of this book, I am going to cover some basic elements of what White supremacy, White supremacy culture, and whiteness are as these topics are embedded in many of the ideas that we have covered up to this point. This book is not about White supremacy. This book is about what to do and how to be an ally that is moving society toward an egalitarian experience. If you are interested in learning more about White supremacy and White supremacy culture and the related history, I recommend reading two books: *In the Matter of Color: Race and the American Legal Process: The Colonial Period* by A. Leon Higginbotham Jr. and *Stamped from the Beginning: The Definitive History of Racist Ideas in America* by Ibram X. Kendi.

White supremacy is the belief that White people are superior to all other races and should therefore dominate society. As we explored in Part I of this book, in American history, White people did dominate other groups and specifically enslaved Black people. The founding of this country was based on White ideals and increasing opportunity for White people, especially White men. Just like building a house, if the foundation is a problem, it impacts the whole house. Having White supremacy as a foundation has created a nation where ideas about White culture and the standards defined by that culture are embedded into the systems we operate with today.

White supremacy culture, also known as whiteness, is the perspective that White people, communities, and culture are superior and are seen as "correct" and valued above others. Here is the thing about culture: When you are a part of it, it is difficult to perceive. It is why we struggle sometimes to see our own privilege and have a hard time identifying when what we are doing is oppressive to others. Culture is a part of identity, and being American is to grow up with whiteness. Standards for what schools are good or bad are based on White ideas, White needs, and White children. Standards for what should be legal or illegal are based on White ideas, White needs, and White perspectives about safety. The media is owned and controlled by White standards. When people go to medical school, the material they learn is almost exclusively based on research done by White men on how medical conditions appear in White people. Medical facilities are primarily White owned and run. When something is good, we whitelist it, as opposed to blacklist—terminology originating from times of mass enslavement that reinforces "White = good" mindsets. In the United States, White is the standard—a standard we often uphold by calling it politically correct, or being respectful, without regard for the many identities not included when we elevate White as the standard.

If you are a White person, this can feel hard to read. You may even want to resist it. I totally understand that. It doesn't feel good to read that an aspect of your identity that you did not choose for yourself can have such a sordid history and be so deeply entrenched in the oppressive experience of others. Remember, though, this discussion isn't personal. We are all living according to the White standard established by White supremacy. Black and Brown communities are also complicit in upholding and normalizing the ideas and practices that are steeped in whiteness. It is hard to break free of something that feels normal because it is a part of your everyday life. But it isn't normal. It isn't equitable. It is just White.

I want to be clear here, I am not suggesting that White people are bad. After all, it isn't just White people who adhere to the whiteness standards. Many identities do, out of a lack of awareness or otherwise. I do experience that many White people are unwilling to consider the possibility that their entire reality has been constructed to assure them comfort, even at the expense of other identities. If you are White, think about it: What if your whole life was created, controlled, and regulated by people who didn't look like you? What if those same people had a history of mistreating people who looked like you? How would you feel about sending your children to schools and medical institutions designed by them? How would you feel if almost all of your child's programming was created by them? How would you feel if you attained legal freedom, access to vote, and the rights to some form of safety only when their legal institutions said so?

There's a lot to unpack with whiteness and White supremacy, but here are the main two things I want you to take from this section:

1. It is highly likely that when you are critical of another human's value, attractiveness, level of education, adherence to social norms, or vernacular, you are doing so with White being the standard.
2. The White standard isn't correct; it just is familiar.

We should all make a concerted effort to consider that another community or culture may do things differently and we may find that process to be unfamiliar. Make a conscious effort to recognize that unfamiliar does not mean incorrect. An example is when people assume that the way Black people speak to each other is improper English and an indicator of lack of education. This is untrue. African American Vernacular English (AAVE), sometimes known as African American English (AAE), is a dialect of English. It is the type of English many Black people speak to one another. It is not wrong, uneducated, or in need of correction.

NOTE: There is a good episode of the *ASHA Voices* podcast about African American English called "Language and Identity—Shifting Away from a Deficit Perspective on African American English" by J. D. Gray. The transcript for the podcast is available at `leader.pubs` `.asha.org/do/10.1044/2020-0227-transvoices-language-identity`.

Antiracism

The term "antiracism" means exactly what it suggests: being against racism. Many times people want to make sure they are not racist, but approaching racism from the perspective of just not participating in it is not an option. As we discussed when we covered the system and -isms, we are all complicit. Not being racist or not believing you are a part of racism does nothing to dismantle the system of racism. Not being racist is not enough. We want allies and advocates who are antiracist, meaning they will take action to interrupt racism.

Just like allyship and advocacy, antiracist is an action word. It means that when a family member does something racist, you actively challenge their thought process, not just remove yourself from the discussion. Antiracist also means fighting against local policies that are racist. It can also mean being intentional about what you expose your children to, from television programming, to books, to toys. Being antiracist isn't just for White people, it is for everyone, because we are all participating in the system of racism. However, White people have more power and influence to change racist policy and practices, and that's why we need White folks to be antiracist too.

Questions to Consider

1. What part of learning about "the system" stood out to you the most?
2. Define in your own words the difference between systemic and systematic.
3. Which -isms currently grant you privilege or favor? How might you be able to use those privileges as an ally?

14

Resistance Language

Many of the terms and concepts we have covered in this section of the book make people angry and they will start to use what I call "resistance language." These are statements of privilege because they give users the opportunity to discount certain issues that some people do not have the option to ignore. Resistance language is usually meant to undermine or redirect away from the topic at hand. Take a scroll through your favorite social media platform and you are prone to see any of these statements or hear something like them:

"Everyone is equal, we are all human."

"I am colorblind."

"This information ignores the challenge experienced by x groups experiencing y struggle."

"But what about the Holocaust?"

"What does this have to do with _____?"

"We should focus on Black-on-Black crime."

"Police kill more White people than Black people."

"I just try to stay neutral."

"All lives matter."

The timing of these statements is usually poor, and they can cause disconnection or set the stage for a debate. Let's not let that happen to us, allies! I want to make sure you understand what these statements are suggesting, why they are not okay to use, and how to respond if they come up in future conversations. Let's visit these in buckets. The first bucket includes these statements:

"Everyone is equal, we are all human."

"I am colorblind."

"I just try to stay neutral."

"All lives matter."

These statements all speak to an ideal. Indeed, we are all human, and in an ideal world, yes, everyone would be equal. Someone's skin color would not matter, and we could all enjoy the harmony of being neutral if all lives mattered. The reality is that many people in underrepresented groups do not experience this ideal. Here are a few potential nonconfrontational but factual responses to resistance language about "an ideal":

"It is ideal that we would all be equal, but reality is very different."

"Although we are all human, some people's human rights have been so oppressed that we have had laws passed to say that they have the same rights as everyone else." The Civil Rights Act of 1964 that we covered in Part I is an example of this. Another example is that the Supreme Court passed a ruling in 2020 that says that LGBTQ people are covered under the Civil Rights Act of 1964.

"Many people of different skin tones are very proud of their heritage and it is an important part of their identity. We should want to see the fullness of people, not just choose the parts we want to see."

The second bucket of resistance language is what I call "the redirect" but is technically known as whataboutism. These statements fall in that bucket:

"This information ignores the challenge experienced by x groups experiencing y struggle."

"But what about the Holocaust?"

"What does this have to do with _____?"

`Merriam-Webster.com` describes whataboutism as a reversal of accusation, arguing that an opponent is guilty of an offense just as egregious or worse than what the original party was accused of doing, however unconnected the offenses may be. These statements may have nothing to do with the topic at hand and are intended to suggest that the conversation should be focused on a perceived "bigger" offense. Here are some responses to "the redirect":

> "I am not ignoring any struggles or information. I recognize that there are many marginalized groups that have suffered. I don't think we need to put historical discrimination and violence in competition with each other."

> "Right now, I am focusing on _____."

The last bucket, which I call "distorted facts," includes the last couple of statements from the earlier list:

> "We should focus on Black-on-Black crime."

> "Police kill more White people than Black people."

I call these distorted facts because they are factual but not the full picture. Black-on-Black crime rates are about the same as White-on-White crime rates because data says people commit crimes in their own communities. So, yes, Black-on-Black crime matters, but it matters because crime matters. Police do kill more White people than Black people because there are more White people in the United States. However, Black people are killed at a higher rate than White people are, meaning the likelihood of being killed by police if you are Black is higher. Sneaky, right? Here are some ways to respond to distorted facts.

> "Black-on-Black crime rates are the same as White-on-White crime rates. Historically, people commit crimes in their own communities."

> "I am focused on risk, not quantity. Since Black people are only about 13% of the population, we need to look at this data differently than by keeping count. Black people have a greater risk of being killed by the police when compared to White people."

> "I understand; right now I am focusing on _____."

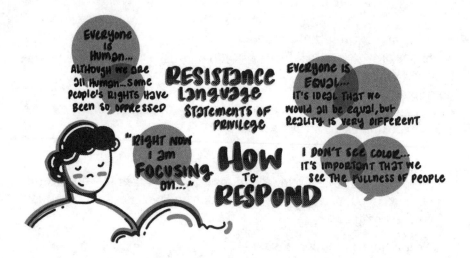

Sometimes you aren't going to know what to say to someone who hits you with resistance language, and that's okay. You always have the option of not engaging in the discussion, especially if it is clear the person would rather argue. I opt out of conversations when I realize someone does not want to have a useful discussion. I realize that it's no one's job to convince people. I prefer to focus on sharing information with those who have a growth mindset and are open to change rather than to spend energy defending ideas to someone who is committed to their own perspective. Feel empowered to end nonproductive discussions respectfully. I usually say "Ah. I hear you. Good chatting!" or something else both polite and to the point that makes it clear I am exiting the conversation. On the off chance the person asks why I am ending the discussion, I say something like "This discussion doesn't feel like the best way to spend my energy right now. I do appreciate you sharing your ideas with me, though."

Questions to Consider

1. What are some resistance language statements you have encountered? How would you react to those statements after reading this chapter?
2. What responses to resistance statements are most helpful for you? Can you come up with a few of your own responses to resistance language?

The Work
Starts with You

Throughout this book we have done activities and explored questions to help shift your mindset toward being an ally to others. We all can fall into the programming and biases that we are surrounded by on a daily basis that can make being an ally feel like a challenge. So in this part of the book, I want to share tactics you can use on your allyship journey, revisit tactics we've discussed to share some additional insight, and share some perspectives that might be helpful.

It is helpful to view equity and inclusion work as a lifestyle change. Think about other lifestyle changes you have taken on in your life. Say you want to get fit or you want to start eating vegan. You begin by determining how you can change your mindset, and then you set about identifying actions you can make a part of your routine every day. Being an ally is the same: You have to work on your mindset first by learning things and understanding the problems. Then you have to commit to making small, incremental habit changes every day that ultimately will make the difference, as with any lifestyle change.

We make the changes we want to see in the world by working on ourselves first. Start with you. As I have stated elsewhere in this book, we are all complicit in upholding the systems that oppress. Even I am guilty of being complicit—and I work in the inclusion and equity space. In the past, I often was willing to soften messages just to get the message across the line for a very nervous client. Instead of using the term "racism," I have said "discrimination," based on someone's race. I'm guilty of creating comfortable, safe experiences for leaders because I was so eager to get at least part of the message to land. I don't do that anymore. I stopped using complicit language. I have stopped softening messages and attempting to make what isn't pretty, comfortable, or nice feel that way. There is always some work I need to do to not uphold systems of oppression. The same is true for you and for everyone.

Examine yourself. Start the work with yourself, your mindset, and your behaviors. As you learn and grow into the lifestyle change, it will become routine for you to stand up, speak up, and push back on injustice. But the work starts with you. What are the practical ways you are going to embed being an ally into your life? In this last section of the book, we explore some ideas that may be good techniques to start with.

When people are introduced to the work of being an ally or the work of inclusion and equity, they usually start out interested and try to learn everything they can. After a while, once they have consumed so much information, occasionally people hit a wall. They start to experience what I call "obstacles to allyship." These obstacles are perspectives that make it difficult to continue doing the work of learning and becoming an effective ally and advocate. Three main mindsets I encounter present as obstacles. Let's explore these perspectives and some ways to address them when they come up.

The first mindset is disbelief, usually marked by people saying something like "I don't believe it." After seeing many things they didn't know were happening to others or learning about some of the types of oppression that others experience, these people get to a point where they say, "No way has all this been going on and I have never seen it. It can't be true," or simply "This cannot be real. I don't believe it."

We have to remember that our reality is not *the* reality. Although we might all be living on the same planet and even in some cases in the same cities, reality is based on lived experience. Try as you might, you can see the world only through your own eyes. Your experience of what is real and what is not is constantly and inextricably tied to your own experience.

The second mindset I encounter with people new to allyship is guilt, which can sound like "I feel so bad/guilty." Typically, this feeling is associated with coming to awareness about the many ways that systems we all participate in are not working well for marginalized people. As I have mentioned a few times, guilt is a normal feeling. Feel your feelings, identify them, but do not allow guilt to paralyze you. We need you to be an ally and an advocate for others.

If you find yourself feeling bad, guilty, or otherwise disappointed, remind yourself that inclusion and equity work is not personal. It is systemic, and we are all complicit in some way. The way to address the issues is to look at the roles we play in supporting systems that uphold racist, antiquated, and discriminatory ideas and practices. There is not a running list of ways that you are complicit, and because our complicity is entrenched in our lives, it can be hard to see. This is why the listening and learning part of being an ally and an advocate is so important. As you learn more, you will begin to notice for yourself the ways life is unjust and to identify ways you can personally, using your privilege, power, and influence, address what you identify.

2. FEELS LIKE A PERSONAL FAILURE

GUILT · SHAME · OVERWHELM ARE V·A·L·I·D... BUT NOT VALID REASONS TO STOP DOING THE WORK

Remember, this work is not about feeling good. It is about you being different in ways that you may have never considered.

The last mindset that presents an obstacle to allyship and advocacy is being overwhelmed, which can sound like "This problem is too big to solve." No doubt about it, inequity and injustice are big problems. As we have explored, they are deeply entrenched in our lives and have been established over many years. The problem is not too big to solve. Solving it just is going to take time, just as it took time to get here. There is no time like the present for you to realize that to get to solve, you need to understand your personal place and power in the problem. Solutions arise as you move through understanding the issues and being able to identify them. Yes, again, I am turning responsibility back on to you, dear reader. You cannot skip right to solve. But you can start working on evaluating the bias in your own perspectives and behaviors toward others. In Chapter 16 we look at some simple tactics to help us open our eyes to invite other viewpoints.

Questions to Consider

1. Have you encountered an obstacle to allyship? If so, which one? Have you been able to move past it?
2. What small practices can you embed into your life to help you make allyship and advocacy a lifestyle change?

16 Role-Modeling Inclusion

Behaving in an inclusive manner helps create a culture of equity and belonging. We have covered a lot of ideas and approaches in this book, but in this chapter, we cover tips and tactics you can use to help you role-model inclusion. We also revisit a few key techniques mentioned earlier in the book to add additional context or resources. There are a lot of ideas and tools to choose from, but don't be overwhelmed. Remember, the work of allyship and advocacy are lifestyle changes and take time. Consider which techniques will fit best in your routine to get started. As you master those techniques, you can begin practicing others.

Broaden Your Perspectives

One way to broaden your perspective is to **consider your unique access**. What is something that only you or a select few others can do or have access to? Maybe you have a unique job. Maybe you make decisions about learning for a specific population. Maybe you have not well-publicized information about how to navigate a certain career field. Your job as an ally and an advocate is to identify how you are uniquely positioned to impact change that creates a culture of belonging—even with the people whose reality you don't entirely understand.

Here's an example. I typically teach corporations and their employees, but, inspired by a mentor and one of my employees, my company decided to host a consumer-facing online course in June 2020. The class was 90 minutes and focused on allyship. About 30 people signed up. One of those people was an editor for John Wiley & Sons, a publishing company. After the class, she sent me a note on Instagram asking if I was open to discuss writing a book. I did three back flips inside and I told her absolutely!

In our first chat, I asked, "What made you reach out to me and see if I was interested in writing a book?" She said, "Well, in that class I took, you said I should consider what I have the power and privilege to do. I have not only the power and the privilege but also the obligation to find new authors. It is my job. Most authors I find are White. Why not you?" That discussion turned into the book you are reading now. I'm still a bit shocked and humbled as I type these words. Consider just how impactful people can be if they just slow down and take a critical look at what they have power over and then decide to do something differently.

Another way to change your perspective is to **enhance your standard**. Standards are everywhere. There are standards to get a job. There are standards for joining organizations. Standards of dress. Standards for behavior. We are swimming in standards and norms. Take a critical look, and you will find that the standards you hold so dear were established for you and are deeply connected to your worldview. Have you ever noticed how White the standards are? Consider fashion, music, entertainment, sports—Black people are definitely the culture creators and leaders in some pretty powerful spaces, yet they are not the beneficiaries of the consumption of that culture. Consider your favorite musicians. Are they classically trained? Did they come from a privileged background and attend all the best schools before making it big? Likely not. In some cases, our favorites are the innovators of a specific sound— here's looking at you, Stevie Wonder. Yet, when someone we care about wants to be a musician, we starting thinking about the standards they need to adhere to and the steps they need to follow and the investment it will take. We do the same thing for jobs—we design education and experience standards that people need to meet in order to be considered fit to do a role. You want a fashion designer job and didn't go to Parsons School of Design or the Fashion Institute of Technology? Good luck.

Ask yourself, "Who gave you that standard you are using? How do you know it is right?"

If you look around and see few (if any) Black, Brown, or Indigenous people, is it possible that the standard is wrong? Or do you think that Black, Brown, or Indigenous people just can't achieve the standard despite being the culture creators for many industries for decades? We have to be willing to consider that we are missing out on talent and relationships and resources and, most importantly, equitable opportunities because we hold people to standards we have not considered being critical of. Sometimes we even hold others to standards that we didn't have to meet ourselves to get to the same position. I know several people who landed jobs because of who they knew and their social networks, but when they evaluate others' talent, they hold them to a higher and more critical standard for the same type of opportunity.

You can change your mind about what the standard is, especially in the realms in which you have influence. Ask yourself: "Is this standard equitable? Is there another way to evaluate fairly? Should we discount someone who is incredibly skilled if they don't meet the standard?" Most importantly, ask yourself: "Who might we be missing because not everyone has access to the opportunity to meet these standards?"

Another way to broaden your perspective is to **intentionally prioritize your discomfort**. As we discussed in Chapter 13, growth comes from discomfort, but many of us do our best to be as comfortable as possible at all times. Comfort is alluring, but it honestly will not help you to continue to have the insight and experiences necessary to be a strong ally and advocate. You have to be willing to speak up even when it feels uncomfortable. You have to be willing to ask respectful and challenging questions to push back against injustice. You have to be willing to do this work even when it feels emotionally scary. You have to be willing to chance saying the wrong thing and to be willing to learn from feedback. You have to be confident enough to apologize and change your behavior. You have to embrace the possibility that someone, even friends or family, may be offended by your allyship. It's not as simple as putting on a Black Lives Matter T-shirt or waving a rainbow flag. You shift your perspective by being willing to bravely manage the encounters that may come when someone disagrees with your BLM shirt. You shift your perspective when you are having uncomfortable conversations with family members about how they see Black people and disabled people and LGBTQ people and whomever you feel strongly about being an ally for. People you care about may be upset with you, and that is uncomfortable and sad. At the same time, you may save someone's life.

I chair an organization called Brown Girls Do Ballet® that was founded in 2013. The organization's purpose is to promote diversity in ballet by providing annual scholarships, a mentor network, and community programs to empower young girls to pursue their love of dance. The founder, TaKiyah Wallace, speaks openly about how everything Brown Girls Do Ballet® does starts with a young dancer willing to be brave and uncomfortable. For perspective, ballet is a very competitive environment in which complicity is rewarded. Young girls risk damaging their careers by speaking up about injustices or even the challenges they face. The young women and girls served by Brown Girls Do Ballet® are some of the bravest people I know because they find ways to speak up, to challenge the status quo, and to push back against injustices while still doing the hard work to advance their careers.

One example of girls speaking up is about pointe shoe colors. Ballet clothing and shoe companies all make ballet shoes in soft pink or soft beige—ballet attire is supposed to blend in with the performer's skin tone. For many years, Black and Brown dancers had to hand-dye their shoes in a process called pancaking. This isn't a one-and-done process as ballet dancers literally dance through their shoes. Professional dancers can easily go through 10 or 15 pairs of shoes a *week*, and shoes average about $90 a pair. Many dancers opted to use foundation makeup to dye their shoes so they could find the right shade, which adds the additional expense of buying the make-up. Not to mention the hour or so necessary to pancake the shoes. Some years ago girls started sharing the process for dying shoes online, and Brown Girls Do Ballet® gave visibility to the tedious process. In videos, dancers started speaking about the expense and time it took to pancake their shoes, a process that White dancers do not have to do for their shoes to match their skin tone. Finally, in 2017, the company Gaynor Minden released pointe shoes in a range of Brown shades. Other brands are slowly starting to offer different shades of shoes too. Though many cannot be ordered online or carry an additional fee for brown satin.

Should you find yourself in the position of resigning to your own comfort, think about the bravery and commitment of Black and Brown ballerinas and their willingness to train hard, be powerful, and make it beautiful—all while still challenging the status quo.

The last tip I want to offer to help you broaden your perspective is to **lean into exposure opportunities**. Comfort can definitely keep us away from exposing ourselves to new things and new people, but so can our preconceived notions about things we are unfamiliar with. Make a point to introduce yourself to different experiences. It doesn't have to be a major thing; it can be something fun that you are skeptical about. For me, it was snowboarding. The very first time I was invited to go snowboarding, I laughed. I imagined myself in the mountains with a bunch of White people, and it sounded like the beginning of a cheesy horror film. My bias made me super skeptical, but because I believe in exposing myself to new things, I went. Let me tell you—snowboarding for the first time in the Poconos is the most fun I have ever had falling down. My assumption that I would only see White people on the mountain? Totally wrong. There were people from all over the world and of all ages skiing and snowboarding. My entire attitude changed after that, and although I am not good at it at all, I'm down to snowboard anytime!

Exposure opportunities can be much smaller acts as well. It can be deliberately grocery shopping in a neighborhood you have made some assumptions about. It can be doing a music exchange with a friend who has different musical tastes than you. It could even be a book or recipe exchange. The point is to expose yourself to things so you can see the world that is hidden from you. Doing this gives you a greater ability to understand your own identity, power, and privilege. I want to mention here that you have to do this with an open mind. You can't approach exposure opportunities through the lens of seeing "what is wrong" with how others think or live. It isn't about showing anyone the "right way" or saving someone from their lives or perspectives. It is about broadening your worldview without adding the layer of judgment or a personal ranking system that says this is better than that.

Be Mindful of Shared Spaces

Throughout this book I refer to spaces as shared spaces. The term "shared spaces" means that you are there with others whom you didn't necessarily invite and with whom you will be using the space collaboratively or simultaneously. These spaces can include openly public spaces, such as parks, museums, and stores, but also spaces that are private or require certain access, such as airports, workplaces, or conferences. Being an ally matters most in these spaces to ensure that people feel included. Everyone should be able to feel welcomed, connected, and safe in their identities in these spaces.

We should work to ensure that in shared spaces people are not mistreated or subject to discrimination or -isms. Some legal parameters exist to ensure treatment in some of these spaces is equitable, such as those set forth by the Equal Employment Opportunity Commission or the American Disabilities Act. We can be mindful of shared spaces by behaving in ways that reinforce that everyone in a shared space has access to an equitable experience rather than focusing only on our individual experience.

Use Gender-Inclusive Language and Examples that Appeal to Varied Interests

Inclusive language is critical to role-modeling allyship. It is one of the ways we can ensure that people are aware that we are committed to ensuring people can share their identities and will be seen and heard. American English and American experiences are very gendered, so sometimes we use the words and examples that we are familiar with instead of thoughtfully and intentionally using inclusive language. What is the most common mistake I hear from people who want to be inclusive?

Guys.

"Hey, guys, let's get started!"

"Guys, we need to think about this as a team."

Even in organizations that I support that are largely women led, I hear the term "guys" constantly, even when there are no males in the room.

Some argue that "guys" and "dude" are gender neutral because women use the terms with each other. Here's the thing: Context and environment matters. When you are with your friends or people with whom you have built strong relationships, say what works. Don't let that delude you into believing that "guys" or "dudes" is gender neutral, though. Consider the following examples:

"How many guys did you date before you met your spouse?"

"How many dudes are coming to the baby shower?"

Do those questions sound gender neutral to you? They don't to me. They suggest a specific gender. Although I can get away with an exaggerated "Girl!" with my men friends when I have something exciting to share or may slide the occasional "Son!" in when I want to make a point, these terms are *not* gender inclusive. Especially now, when the concept of gender is evolving from binary male/female to a spectrum of identity, it's helpful to use terms that do not connote any specific gender.

Alternative words to use include:

- Everyone
- Folks—sometimes spelled folx

- Peeps
- Friends
- Colleagues
- Y'all
- Pals
- People
- Squad
- Team
- Leaders

You'll also want to avoid the word "tribe" in shared spaces. This term can be offensive to Native American people, who may view it as an anthropological term or as a word that uniquely belongs to their indigenous community. It is not universally offensive, but it can be. Remember when we are thinking about language, who says what matters. How things are said matters. The word "tribe" is one of those terms that can easily offend certain audiences, so let's avoid it, especially in shared spaces.

Gender slips into our language in other ways as well. Consider the next word replacements to make gendered terms neutral:

Instead of . . .	Use . . .
Busboy	Kitchen helper
Cameraman	Camera operator
Congressman	Congressperson
Foreman	Foreperson or crew leader
Ladies and Gentlemen	Everyone or distinguished guests
Policeman	Police officer
Postman	Mail carrier or postal person
Salesman	Salesperson
Stewardess	Flight attendant

It's not about taking terms that are masculine and making them feminine. It is about being neutral. Our goal in shared spaces is to create an opportunity for everyone to see they can belong, so we want to lean neutral with our language.

Another place gender can show up is with the references or examples we use. Take a look at the following sentences;

"I can't wait until we know who our new leader will be. I hope she is a strong developer of talent."

"Let's set up a meeting so we can figure out how to quarterback this thing."

The first sentence suggests that the new leader will be female. Why do we do this? Lots of reasons rooted in our bias, which, as you may recall, happens in our brains, often outside of our control. Remember, we are always biasing all over, everywhere. Try to be mindful of times you suggest gender when speaking to others.

The second sentence uses a football reference. As awesome as football is, everyone doesn't know what a quarterback is or does. What if you work for a global company and many team members have no idea what a quarterback does in American football? Speaking of American football, only men play professionally, so the experience of being a quarterback is largely exclusively male (although women do play in amateur leagues in the United States). Also, not everyone enjoys or connects to sports references, just like everyone doesn't enjoy the same type of music. Try to use examples that a wide variety of audiences can connect to regardless of their location in the world or their gender.

You'll notice that a lot of the examples I list in this section are male. The reason is that more male gender noninclusive terms are used commonly than female terms. You may be able to think of some ways that language that skews female is also gender exclusive. There is nothing wrong with looking for more references. Remember, though, the objective is to move away from gender when speaking in shared spaces.

Demonstrate Equality

In Chapter 10 we talked about the difference between equity and equality and how there is a place for both. An ally makes a pointed effort to determine when a situation calls for equity, equality, or a mix of the two. However, when we are thinking about teaming with and leading others, equality should be on our minds. We want to ensure that we are not showing favoritism or treating people differently, especially based on a diversity attribute. Consider the next example:

Talia was newly promoted to the executive team. She was excited about her new role as executive vice president of Marketing and being able to build relationships with the rest of the executive team. She expected that she was going to have to work a little to build relationships with the all-male team, but she was ready for the challenge. Besides, they selected her for the role, so it couldn't be so bad. Six weeks in, she noticed that, despite her best efforts, she didn't really feel connected to the team. After asking a few mentors and friends for advice, she started paying attention to the ways the other leaders were connecting with each other.

Talia noticed that early in the mornings before everyone got down to business, she would be in her office getting ready for the day and she'd hear a few members of the executive team in the office next to hers talking and laughing. She could only make out small parts of the conversations, but it was enough to know they were not about work but friendly chatter. After another week or so, Talia decided one morning to walk over to the office and join the conversation. As she enters the doorway everyone falls silent, so she nervously says hello to what amounts to most of the executive team. The CEO clears his throat and says, "Good morning, Talia. My apologies if we are too loud." Talia bravely says, "No, not at all. But I wanted to come over and see if I could join in on whatever you all found so funny this morning." She smiles. The CEO looks around the room then back at Talia and says, "Wow, I'm so sorry we didn't invite you over. We've been working together so long, I didn't even realize it," and he motions for her to have a seat. A few seconds later, the conversation picks back up and Talia finally feels like she is building a connection with her new team.

Do you think the executive team meant to leave Talia out? Likely not. Sometimes our routines can blind us to the ways we are treating some people differently from others. Demonstrating equality in team environments lets people know that everyone on the team has the same value and will be treated fairly. It lets people know that favoritism does not have a place in the team environment. It also requires that we pay attention so we don't slip into behaviors similar to the one the executive team did. Imagine if Talia had not decided to say anything. Imagine if the CEO had not realized what message he and the rest of the team were sending. Remember, being inclusive takes work; anticipate mistakes along the way. Also, sometimes we have to do the brave thing and speak up for ourselves even when it seems unfair. Talia should not have had to take the initiative to start the discussion, but when people don't see their own bias, we can help them see it by stepping up and taking action. I speak more about doing the brave thing later in this chapter.

The failure to treat people equally also shows up in passing encounters. Consider that one friend who always seems annoyed with restaurant staff but treats the restaurant owner with the utmost respect. Think about how you greet the custodial staff you encounter versus the executive you find yourself riding the elevator with everyday. I am not suggesting that you treat every person you encounter with the same care you lend to your closest friends and family. I am suggesting that you should treat everyone with equal courtesy and respect, regardless of their job title or their station in life.

Do the Brave Thing

I tell my mentees all the time to do the brave thing. There are times when we all are faced with the choice between holding our tongues or pushing back against inequity. Many times we decide not to speak up and to just deal with it and vow to not be in that position again. Think about how many times have you suffered bad service and simply said to yourself, "I just won't be back." Many times we will not speak up for ourselves, let alone speak up for others. We aren't brave. We shy away from challenging discussions and unfair treatment, often out of fear of confrontation. What we fail to consider is that the person who treats us poorly will continue, often obliviously, to mistreat others. There might be a part of you that says "At least it is not me," but what if it is someone you care about? What if it is someone who makes decisions that impact you? For any of us to ever get out from the weight of systemic oppression, we must do the brave thing.

Even working in the inclusion and equity space, there are times when doing the brave thing is a challenge. In the months following the murder of George Floyd, my consulting company, Cabral Co., received a large number of requests for support from various industries. One request came from a company that seriously lacked racial and ethnic diversity in their workforce and generally had not prioritized equity in their workplace. After an initial call, we shared a proposal with pricing for the company to review.

A day or so later, the potential client sent an email with a few questions and an offer that said: "Would you potentially consider a marketing advertisement package on our platform in lieu of payment? We could expose your business to millions of customers. As we are still a not-yet-profitable start-up, I wanted to see if we can be creative to pay for these services."

Because we are a business, my staff replied in kind. They did not address the problems with the message at all; instead, they professionally stated that the offer did not align with what we have done in the past, but we are open to future discussion to see what we can work out. Hours later in a debrief, my staff brought the message to my attention and added, "Don't worry, we have taken care of it."

Honestly, the potential client's email was a problem, but my larger concern was that my staff was not brave in their response. I immediately jumped in and sent a respectful but also very clear message to the potential client stating three things:

1. No company should be comfortable with the optics of asking a very small, Black-owned business to exchange work for social media ads.
2. Exchanging ad share for work directly seems incredibly out of touch in light of the times (although I realize that no harm may have been intended).
3. Women, Black people, and other marginalized groups are often underresourced, undercompensated, and meet with significantly higher risks when running their own businesses. Underscoring a commitment to racial equity, diversity, and inclusion goes beyond hiring someone. It also means using your influence to dismantle structural and institutional racism, starting with paying marginalized people and groups fairly and equitably for their labor.

I ended the email by sharing that I realize Cabral Co. will likely no longer be a candidate for partnership, given my candor. However, as a company, Cabral Co. cares too much about this work and this world to not shed some light on the incredible risk to their organization by taking the approach of exchanging labor for ads. Cabral Co. is also keenly aware of the oppressive systems reinforced by not speaking up about why asking to exchange work for ads is not equitable.

I wanted the client. I could have been nice and courteous and simply left our response to the exchange at "No, we will not accept ads as payment." It wasn't about the method of payment, though. It was about ensuring that anyone else who deals with that organization will not encounter the same experience. I had to do the brave thing.

We didn't land the gig. Ultimately, the person who sent the email apologized and said they understood how the request came across poorly. We even had a follow-up discussion. I believe my message was received, and I hope that whomever the company selected to work with did not face a similar inappropriate request.

Sometimes doing the brave thing means being willing to engage in tough conversations with people we care about, such as close friends, parents, or even spouses. In fact, allyship and advocacy behaviors should start with those you are closest to. Is it going to be uncomfortable to tell your uncle that he shouldn't call gay people faggots? Absolutely. Might he get upset with you? It is definitely possible. You still should do it because you have the credibility, because of your relationship to actually be heard. Your uncle might be upset, but you never know—he might never discuss it with you again but will think twice about his word choice in how he engages with others. Start with your immediate circle to build your bravery. Likely it will feel the most emotionally challenging, but it also will have the most impact.

Seek Out Diversity

Some people are put off by the idea of being intentional about diversity, especially when we are talking about hiring people. It is imperative that we intentionally seek out diversity because we do not naturally attract it. The way we have been socialized is that we are attracted to people who are similar to us or have a similar worldview as us. As a result, diversity does not tend to naturally occur. People apply to jobs where they have friends. People attend parties where they know the guests. People attend schools where there are children like their children. Men are often assigned to stock shelves in stores while women are asked to dress the windows. We subconsciously look for younger people for tech jobs rather than people who are older with more experience. None of this means you are a bad person, but it is not allyship behavior either. Allies who want to diversify have to be to be intentional.

One tactic you can use to help you diversify is to always ask the question "Who is missing?" Starting a project, who is missing on the project team? Looking to hire for a new role, take note if your talent slate is all male or all female, and ask your HR partners to diversify. Allies are intentional about making sure a diverse selection of people is represented, even in their personal spaces. Similarity bias causes us to surround ourselves with people who are like us, which is a source of groupthink and closes off opportunity for us to grow. Likely, as you are reading this paragraph, you are thinking about the diversity of people in your own life. Consider the next questions:

- Have you ever been the only one like you in the room?
- How frequently do you enter a room and are the only person like you? Do you notice? What thoughts or feelings arise when this situation occurs? What do you think others might think or feel?

Some years ago I was working with a White male leader who was the executive sponsor for the African American networking group. The group's chair asked the man if he would deliver the message introducing the program, to which he agreed. I accompanied him to the meeting, and he gave a great opening message. As soon as we walked out of the room, he let out a long sigh and said, "Whew! I was the only one in there!" I stopped walking and looked right at him. He turned beet red. Here he was, a White man who was uncomfortable being the only White man in the room, and said so to me, a Black woman. He launched into an apology and I stopped him. "No need to apologize. What I want is for you to remember this feeling. Remember the sigh and the feeling of relief you just had leaving that room. Imagine if that was your work world every single day. That is the motivation I want you to carry into supporting this networking group because the people in that room feel that way every time they walk into this building."

When asked to think of the diversity in our lives, typically we can think of a few folks we know, maybe not that well. Do you actually have meaningful relationships with people who are different from you?

Remember in Chapter 8 when I asked you to pull out a sheet of paper and list ten people you trust who are not immediate family? Find your list. Then fill out the Trust Test form. It's okay to skip areas that you're not sure of.

TRUST TEST

Name	Gender	Race/ Ethnicity	Age	Sexual Orientation	Education	Marital Status M or S	Disability Y or N

Here's the thing: You trust who you trust. I am not telling you that you should not trust the people you put on this list. I am saying that often our circles are not as diverse as we think. If you want to be an ally, it might be worth finding ways to diversify your own life first. Make mental note of the consistencies. Do you list a lot of people of one specific race or ethnicity? Do you know any people who are not heterosexual? What about people with disabilities? The first time I did this, I realized all the people I trusted were Black, and I didn't have anyone I trusted who didn't have an advanced degree. I felt a little embarrassed about it, but I was grateful to have it put in my face that way.

Practice Perspective Taking

Perspective taking is something we have all likely heard before. It means that when you encounter someone who has an opinion that differs from or challenges yours, you make a conscious effort to put yourself in their shoes and try to see things from their perspective. We usually say "I see your perspective" or "I understand" when we recognize someone else's point of view. Too often, though, the sentiment isn't true, and what people actually mean when they say "I see your perspective" is: "I am ready to share my own thoughts on what you said now." What follows is usually a countering perspective or some message that reveals that no point of agreement has been reached. Stop doing this to people. Perspective taking is a great way to actually connect to people who and ideas that are different from yours. It doesn't require agreement; it simply means you are doing the work to see someone else's point of view. And believe me, if you are doing it correctly, it is work. Let me show you what I mean.

Next is a short story about Fabrice. Read the bio and then pretend you are the person described in the story.

My name is Fabrice. I am 35 years old. I was born on a small Caribbean island called Martinique. I spent my teenage years in the United States living just outside of Atlanta, Georgia, with my parents and my younger sister and brother. I went to college and then went to school to become a lawyer. I passed the bar in Georgia and started practicing law in Atlanta. Many of my clients were tried for relatively minor crimes, but occasionally I would get a serious case to defend. Last year I quit practicing law. It started out as a break because my wife and I had a miscarriage, but I couldn't go back. It was just too sad. Plus, I have always been really good at tennis, so a couple years ago, I started teaching tennis part time to children and I loved it! Now I am a full-time tennis coach. I even have a couple of Olympic candidates who practice with me. My biggest complaint these days is when the courts are too wet to practice.

Now read and react to the following four situations as if you are Fabrice.

1. Fabrice and his wife head to a local pub for a bite, and one of the bar televisions is tuned in to *Law & Order*.
   - How does Fabrice feel?
   - What does Fabrice think?
2. Fabrice has a full day of classes tomorrow. He checks the weather in Atlanta before heading to bed and realizes that it's going to be 95 degrees and sunny.
   - How does Fabrice feel?
   - What does Fabrice think?
3. After a few months of trying to conceive, Fabrice's wife tells him that she is pregnant again.
   - How does Fabrice feel?
   - What does Fabrice think?
4. A potential tennis client who has just moved to Atlanta from Paris, France, reaches out about tennis classes for their children. The potential client shares, "I hope it is okay, my children know a little English, but they primarily speak French."
   - How does Fabrice feel?
   - What does Fabrice think?

If you did the activity correctly, this exercise takes a little bit of effort—unless you happen to be a trained actor or actress who is used to adopting character traits. Taking someone else's perspective successfully requires that you have some understanding of others' thoughts, feelings, motivations, and intentions. It is also helpful to have some background information about the other person or be able to make some smart guesses about their background and or how they experience the world.

Sometimes we do not know enough about a person we are speaking to; then the only way we can learn someone's point of view is by listening to what they share with us. In this case, getting a full picture that lets us put ourselves in their shoes means we may need to ask some probing questions about what they are sharing.

Here's another easy demonstration of why perspective taking is important. What number is in the next image?

Now turn the book upside down. What number do you see?

Seeing other's perspectives, even if we do not agree, helps us develop empathy and connection to a perspective other than our own. It grows our mindset so we can connect to the possibility that someone else who has experienced life differently than we have may need something different from what we need for ourselves.

What You Allow, You Teach

At times, we are tempted not to speak up when we see behaviors that are less than ideal for creating inclusive experiences. Maybe we are tired, maybe it means challenging an authority figure we respect, or we may just feel that it doesn't concern us. Allowing noninclusive behaviors that are harmful to others to continue without addressing the poor behavior can create a much larger problem. Not only are we teaching the culprit that poor behavior will be tolerated, but we are also teaching those around us who are watching, such as children or colleagues, where boundaries end.

I used to work on a team where a team member let everyone know he preferred to be called Dez. One of Dez's peers, Kyle, learned his first name was actually Deshi, so he began calling him Deshi, in a very exaggerated way. Dez would introduce himself in a meeting as Dez, and Kyle would chime in, "His real name is Deshi, so I call him Deshi." Eventually several members of the team referred to Dez as Deshi, even though he always introduced himself as Dez. Deshi never said anything, but it was clear he didn't like being called by his given name. He also didn't enjoy being made a spectacle of in introductions to others. At one point, Dez tried to correct what people called him, but many team members didn't take him seriously and even said "No, I want to call you by your real name." Once I realized Dez wanted to be called Dez, I started to correct people in meetings when they referred to him as Deshi. I'd say something like "He prefers to be called Dez" and then continue the discussion as normal. I'd submit the correction when Dez was in the room and when he wasn't. Over time, the team stopped calling him Deshi and referred to him as he preferred. Some team members even began to also correct people who called him Deshi.

Sometime later, Dez pulled me aside to thank me for helping with his name. He explained he likes his given name, but most Americans say it incorrectly, so he prefers Dez in general settings outside of family. Dez also shared that he thought that not saying anything when Kyle first began calling him Deshi, that the novelty would wear off, but it progressed until I started correcting people to call him Dez.

There are a few key learnings to take from this story. First, be mindful of silent collusion: when not saying anything suggests poor behavior is okay. Even unintentionally, you can be teaching people that noninclusive behaviors are acceptable. Dez not speaking up created a bigger issue for a while than if he had spoken up about his name sooner.

Next, don't hesitate to enroll an ally to correct poor behavior. One person saying "Hey, that's not okay" is good, but two is better. Ten is even better. Allies can help teach and role-model the correct behavior to influence those around them, just as how I started saying Dez's name correctly and correcting when people called him Deshi.

The behaviors around what you allow, you teach go hand in hand with the skills we discussed in Chapter 3 about speaking up and giving feedback. **Saying something when you see or hear something that is inappropriate**, especially if it is in a space you engage in frequently, such as with friends or family or in the workplace, is ally and advocate behavior. Even when whatever occurred has not happened to you, speaking up teaches others how to behave inclusively. Remember, you can use a subtle approach, as asking: "Can you say that again, please?" Or you can use a direct approach: "Our colleague said he prefers to be called Dez." Just remember, if you opt to say nothing, you are teaching people that their behavior is okay.

Carry the Spirit of Apology

I introduced how to apologize in Chapter 3, and I want to revisit apologies because apologizing is such an important skill for navigating life. Mistakes are going to happen as everyone is living their lives navigating systems and biasing all over, everywhere. When you carry the spirit of apology, it means you are willing and prepared to deliver a meaningful apology.

An apology includes two parts:

1. I apologize for _____.
2. Moving forward I will _____.

"I apologize for assuming your family is from another country. Moving forward I will not assume things about someone's culture because of their last name."

Sometimes we know we have offended, but we don't really know what the moving-forward action should be. You may realize you offended someone by calling them "exotic" but not understand why it was offensive. You may even have intended it as a compliment. There is a way to apologize for that too.

"I apologize for calling you exotic. Can you please help me understand why it is offensive so I know how to engage in the future?"

Resist the urge to tell people "Well, I didn't mean it offensively," or "What I was trying to say was . . ." Lead with the apology, ask the question, then stop talking. If the person is comfortable they will tell you: "You may find my features interesting or unusual, but when you call someone exotic it feels objectifying and suggests I am from somewhere else." Hearing their response might lead to a really productive learning discussion and possibly build some connectivity if you attentively listen and engage responsibly. Other times the person you offended doesn't want to engage, and they may simply say something like "I find it offensive and that should be enough." To such a response, you can reply, "I understand and I apologize for calling you that. I will not do it again." Remember, as we learned in Chapter 8 on identity, we should call people what they want to be called. Later you can easily do a Google search to find out why something is offensive. Often there is plenty of information online. In the moment, though, lean bravely into an authentic apology and go from there.

An apology is not conditional. So avoid "I'm sorry if I offended you" type statements. There are no "ifs" or "buts" in genuine apologies. Apologizing is about you recognizing you made a mistake and taking ownership of it with an apology. If you are not ready to apologize genuinely, then hold your tongue. People can sniff out a disingenuous apology a mile away.

Sometimes I hear from women who are worried about carrying the spirit of apology because a lot of data says that women tend to apologize too much. I understand that. I am a woman who is definitely prone to apologize my very existence away at times. Here is what I recommend: Use the model I just provided to determine whether an apology is called for. It sounds really silly when you try to apologize by saying something that isn't really an apology but is instead intended to extend courtesy. Consider these examples:

"I apologize for being late. Moving forward I will not get stuck in traffic again."

"I apologize I didn't see you carrying boxes. Moving forward I make sure I am watching so I can help."

These incidents are more being overcourteous and don't warrant apologies so they don't fit well in the model. Of course you will get stuck in traffic again. Instead of apologizing for being late, say, "Thanks for your patience." Instead of "I'm sorry I didn't see you carrying boxes," say, "I'm happy to help you. Please let me know next time so I can assist."

Don't Rely on Spokespeople

I can't begin to tell you how many of my Black friends have shared how they suddenly have become the go-to person for everything diversity with their White friends and colleagues. Many of them are calling me, saying "Amber, I have no idea what to tell these people. They think I know the answers to fix everything just because I am Black." If you are doing this to someone in your life, you are using them as a spokesperson. You may not know it, but they are likely exhausted with you. Step back.

As I shared in Chapter 3, there is no one gay person who speaks for all gays, no one disabled person who speaks for everyone with a disability, no one White woman who speaks for all White women. **Do not rely on someone to be a spokesperson** based on an aspect of their identity. Your go-to colleague or friend also cannot tell you everything there is to know about racial justice or transpeople or how to solve for inequity in an actionable way over the next three weeks. The way to be an ally is to do the work of getting to know people. Recognize that their identities and cultures are as layered as you see your own. Although a few universal truths exist in terms of behaviors that would offend most members of any given community, there is no magic formula to avoid saying the wrong thing. You learn as you build connections with others, sometimes through making mistakes and apologizing along the way.

Avoid Performative Allyship and Advocacy

As we discussed in Chapter 3, performative allyship and advocacy occurs when someone with power and privilege professes support and solidarity with a marginalized group publicly in a way that isn't helpful, is not backed up with meaningful actions, or actively harms that group. Performative allyship or advocacy rewards someone for doing or being good. The reward can be real acknowledgment or virtual likes online. Performative actions give the appearance of improvement, but there is no real impact.

Because performative allyship and advocacy is easy to slip into, ask yourself a few questions to help you determine if you are performing or being impactful.

- What impact will my action have?
    Ideally the action you are taking will make a meaningful impact. It gives money, invests time, holds someone accountable to be equitable, calls for change. If your action does not have an impact on a real problem an underrepresented group faces, it is likely performative.

■ Am I able to see, own, and explain my personal responsibility in this system?

　　We discussed systems of oppression in Chapter 12 and 13, so you should be able to identify a system that is impacting the group you are serving as an ally or an advocate for and be able to identify what role you play in that system. Allies and advocates know they are not perfect and recognize they are a part of the problem. Part of destroying the problem is admitting our place in it.

■ Is my action about me feeling good or being seen as good?

　　Don't get caught up in your desire for comfort. Allyship and advocacy require us to be willing to be uncomfortable and take brave steps. If your action only feels good or only results in people seeing you as doing a good job, is it making a real impact? Some allyship behaviors might feel good and might be visible, but they also require brave and bold actions that will challenge and make progress as well.

Mind Your Micros

In Chapter 9 we discussed microaggressions as small or subtle behaviors that occur in casual encounters that judge, accuse, demean, marginalize, or show prejudice toward someone. Often the microaggressions are based on a part of a person's identity, such as age, race, or gender. Microaggressions can be deliberate or unintentional. Allies and advocates mind their microaggressive behaviors and do their part to address them when they arise. Let's explore some tactics to handle microaggressions.

What If I Overhear or Witness a Microaggression?

First, identify what message the microaggression is sending; doing this helps you to know how to address it. In Chapter 9 we listed some common microaggressions and what they are messaging to the recipient. Once you can identify what message the microaggression is sending, you should speak up. You can say something subtle, such as "I'm not sure I follow your meaning." Alternatively, you can say something direct: "I find what you said inappropriate and offensive, I'd like to share why." Another alternative is to ask a question: "Did you mean to suggest that Tony doesn't look like he is from this country?" Or perhaps: "What do you mean Bianca doesn't look like a lesbian?" Don't just let a microaggression slide. Be brave and speak up, even if you do so in private rather than in a group setting. If you are in the workplace, you may need leadership support. Share with your leader what you heard or saw and why you are concerned about it. If you do address the microaggression privately, make sure you explain why you didn't feel comfortable addressing it in the moment.

What If I Behave Microaggressively?

If you behave microaggressively toward someone, it is the perfect time to put apologizing into practice. You are going to make mistakes, and you will commit microaggressions. You gain so much opportunity, connectivity, and respect when you are willing to ask for forgiveness and know how to meaningfully apologize. We covered how to apologize in Chapter 3 and earlier in this chapter.

As an example, perhaps you reach out to touch a pregnant colleague's baby bump, and she steps out of your reach. You should say "I apologize for attempting to touch your stomach. Moving forward I will be considerate about how my behavior is not considerate of your personal space."

It is not about what you meant, how you intended to come across, or if you would have been offended by the microaggression. What is important is that you recognize the offense and take steps to correct it, starting with an apology.

What If I Am the Recipient of a Microaggression?

Speak up for yourself and let the person know you are offended or uncomfortable. Just as when you overhear a microaggression, it is helpful to identify for yourself what message the microaggression is sending, so you can address it.

For example, imagine you are one of two Latinas on your team. Your name is Ana and the other woman's name is Dora. Several people on your team continue to call you Dora's name and to call her Ana. This is a microaggression because it suggests that you and Dora do not have your own identities because you are both part of the same community. To address it, you might say, "I notice you continue to call me Dora and call the other Latina on our team, Dora, by my name. Can you help me understand why?" Alternatively, you could say, "I'm confused. Do you mean to give Dora this information instead of me?" Both approaches cause the person who committed the microaggression to take note of their behavior so they can correct it.

Should you have to do this labor? No. Unfortunately, in the spirit of what you allow, you teach, speaking up is the first step in getting people to see their microaggressive behaviors and holding them accountable for changing them.

I want to remind you here that you will be working on creating an inclusive experience for others for many years to come. The many steps, tactics, and examples we have covered throughout this book are intended to help you to navigate your journey to allyship and advocacy, but you will make mistakes. Fortunately, you now have a number of tools to draw from to help you recover when you do and turn your missteps into learnings. The more you practice, the easier and more natural showing up as an ally and advocate will become.

Questions to Consider

1. What inclusivity behaviors do you already do well? Think of your own example of when one of the role-modeling inclusivity techniques in this chapter might apply.
2. What inclusive behaviors are you going to commit to practicing over the next 30 days? How will you hold yourself accountable?

Taking Care of Yourself

This closing chapter is about taking care of your well-being while doing the work of allyship and advocacy. As I have stated many times in this book, inclusion and equity work is labor. You will feel all the feelings as you learn to be an ally and an advocate. It is emotional and always evolving. There is ample opportunity to exhaust yourself with conversations, new learning material, or keeping up with the disturbing news stories. You may even be tempted to give up. Don't. We need you! Instead, as with any lifestyle change, you should plan on having some tools and techniques you can use to help you push through tough days and recharge. It will take practice and energy to continue fighting against injustice and work toward an equitable world. Before we jump into techniques to recharge, let's address a few possible concerns you might have about being an ally and an advocate.

I'm Still Worried

Even armed with all the information we have covered in this book, it is possible you are still feeling a little concerned. It is common to feel nervous about any new undertaking, and I am used to hearing a few specific concerns after delivering a training session about allyship. Perhaps you are experiencing one of the concerns listed below.

What If I Am Not Sure What to Say?

Imagine someone you want to support or be an ally for is having a challenging time. For example, I remember vividly the days after George Floyd's murder; many Black Americans were emotionally spent. An ally may want to reach out but be unsure how to engage. If you are not sure what to say, lead with that statement: "I am not sure what to say." Then follow the remark with a sentiment about what you observe, not how you feel. This approach lets the person you are speaking to know that you are at a loss for words, but you are aware there is something impactful happening and it has your attention and concern.

What If I Say the Wrong Thing?

There is no "what if." You absolutely will say the wrong thing at some point. The very nature of interacting with people raises the possibility of offending someone. It is best to prepare yourself for the possibility that you will offend someone, so remember to carry the spirit of apology. We've discussed apologies a few times in this book. Flip back to Chapter 3 or Chapter 16 to revisit how to apologize in a meaningful way. When you say something that offends someone, apologize sincerely and work to correct the behavior. Many people will pardon your behavior if they believe you did not intend to offend and if your apology seems genuine. However, it is always possible that someone may choose not to accept your apology; that is their choice.

How Do I Ensure People Know I Am Being Authentic?

Authenticity is communicated by consistency of behavior and doing what you say you will do. It is possible that you will encounter people that will meet your allyship with skepticism. That's okay. If you mean it, you continue to show up as an ally and operate with integrity. Over time, people learn who folks are by what they do consistently. Besides, the best way to communicate authenticity is to actually be authentic and let who and how you are speak for itself.

How Can I Continue to Learn Without Burdening Anyone?

Learning is a lifelong process. To continue learning, make a commitment to a growth mindset. You continue to learn by taking ownership of your own learning about inclusion, equity, allyship, and advocacy. Learning happens in many forms—by listening to others, doing your own research, or even making sure to lean into new experiences.

Taking control of your own learning can turn your basic and burdensome questions into meaty conversation starters. It takes questions like "What can I do to help?" and turns them into "I want to help by making a donation to an organization that will support the health of Black womxn. I have narrowed it down to two organizations; do you have any thoughts about either of these two organizations?" That last question isn't burdensome; it is meaty and interesting to talk about.

Recharging

Sometimes recharging is not about managing interactions with others with grace but, instead, filling our own tank. One practice that has worked really well for me is sandwiching my day. The first hour of my day and the last hour of my day belong to me. I make sure to start my morning in a way that works for me. Usually that means playing a couple podcasts and maybe taking a morning bath. I don't speak to anyone if I don't want to, and I don't engage with work in any meaningful way. Then, I follow the same practice of ending my day in a way that works for me. Sometimes that is a glass of wine on the roof of my apartment building. Other evenings I curl up with a good book. This routine has assured me of one thing that matters a lot to me: My day will start well and end well.

I realize not everyone has an hour at the top and bottom of their day to dedicate to themselves, especially as we are navigating life around a global pandemic, but try to find some time. Maybe for you it is 15 minutes in the morning and 30 minutes before bed. Make a commitment to give yourself time to feel how you want to feel for a brief period every single day. Doing this can make a big difference in your energy levels over time.

The last tip for staying recharged is to prioritize your own learning and your own behavior change. One of the biggest sources for burnout that I see is people spinning their wheels trying to convince others that equity and inclusion work is important. Learn when you should focus your energy inward and on your own development instead of educating uninvested strangers. As you progress on your allyship and advocacy journey, you will begin to identify pretty quickly whether a conversation is worth the emotional labor or if you are better off conserving your energy. I don't mean that every conversation that is met with some resistance is not worth having, but there will be some conversations that are worth leaning into and others that are not. Conserve your energy by determining when you should or should not engage in discussions with others while always making your own learning and unlearning the priority.

Moving Forward

Throughout this book, we have looked at many ways to approach, engage, and disarm complex conversations and encounters across challenging topics. I have suggested that you practice a few behaviors so they become habits. Identifying your go-to techniques helps you navigate the unexpected. When an opportunity for you to be an ally or an advocate arises, you won't be stunned by the situation and kicking yourself later, saying "Why didn't I say or do something?" Instead, you will bravely lean in and support. Just reading this book is not enough; you have to continue to learn, to expose yourself to different ideas and perspectives, and to actually put the techniques into practice so they will be ready for use. If you haven't done so already, pick a couple of behaviors that jumped out at you in this book and commit to practicing them and learning more.

At times you will want to get angry at someone for their inequitable behavior, or someone may be angry with you. Since this work is all about our identities, not taking things personally is a regular challenge you will encounter—either in yourself or with someone you are speaking with. Whenever I find myself getting upset or realize that the person I am speaking with is upset, I always ask myself, "How would I handle this if it were my little sister?" I use my little sister in this instance because she is the one person I love more than anything and I would do anything in the world to protect her. When someone is angry with me and I want to get angry back, I ask myself, "How would I handle this if it were my little sister?" Doing so changes my whole approach to the discussion. The tactic works both ways too. If I am getting frustrated with someone, I again ask myself: "How would I handle this if it were my little sister?" Usually I can adjust my temperament and manage or exit the encounter with grace. Who is that person for you? Who gives you that extra energy to make things right when you are frustrated? That's who you should use when you ask yourself the question "How would I handle this if . . ."

Allyship and advocacy are the actions many marginalized people need to experience the value, support, and connectedness that we all deserve. Both require that you go further than social media posts and passing check-ins and take steps to change the policies you have influence over or redirect resources into marginalized communities. Allyship and advocacy require you to consider the possibility that your normal is oppressive and your fair is unjust. Being a champion for equity invites you to rise to create opportunities, increase access, grant safety, and, most importantly, save lives. When you, me, and all of us with any sort of power and privilege lean in, we can impact how generations after us experience life, joy, and security in their own skins and identity. The work is challenging and lifelong, but the soul-filling returns are completely worth it.

Thank you for taking this journey with me. I hope this book is useful both as a stimulating read and as a good reference. Mostly, though, I hope that in these pages you have found the confidence and eagerness to authentically lean into making a priority of serving as an ally and an advocate for your fellow people.

Go forth and be brave.

About
the Author

Amber Cabral is an Inclusion and Equity Strategist focused on helping organizations of various sizes and across many industries achieve sustainable leadership and inclusion objectives. She is the founder and principal consultant at Cabral Co., where her work has touched thousands of people, including Fortune 500 executives and senior leaders at global and multinational organizations. Amber is best known for delivering respectful, authentic, and no-nonsense training, strategies, and content that is rich with simple but impactful steps and eye-opening insights that inspire behavior change.

Amber holds a bachelor's degree in psychology with a minor in sociology from Wayne State University and has a master's in organizational leadership and management from Siena Heights University, where she completed her thesis research project on andragogy (adult learning theory). She was formerly a lead for corporate diversity and inclusion initiatives at Blue Care Network of Michigan, where she spent eight years in service and support roles of progressive responsibility. She later served as a leader in Global Talent Management and a senior strategist on the Global Culture, Diversity, and Inclusion team at Walmart Stores, Inc. She has experience with developing and executing company-wide training and strategies to achieve transformational culture change and to embed diversity objectives and inclusive behaviors into the employee life cycle. Today, through Cabral Co., Amber partners with organizations that see the value in improving representation, education, access, and opportunity for marginalized people to bring those goals to life.

Amber's passion for culture and people development extends beyond her professional role as well. She serves as the board chair of Brown Girls Do®, best known for its ballet arm, Brown Girls Do Ballet®, an organization committed to promoting diversity in the arts, such as ballet, by providing annual scholarships, a mentor network, dancer resources, and community programs to empower young women and girls.

Originally from Detroit, Michigan, Amber currently resides in the Washington, DC, metropolitan area. In her free time, she writes articles focused on race, culture, and working-class life, hosts a podcast called *You Can Have Whatever You Want*, and consumes copious hours of audiobooks. She also loves traveling to explore the history and cultural identity of people and nations around the globe.

Index